Y0-DWB-839

The Penalty of Death

The Penalty
of Death

The Canadian Experiment

C.H.S. Jayewardene
University of Ottawa

Lexington Books
D.C. Heath and Company
Lexington, Massachusetts
Toronto

Library of Congress Cataloging in Publication Data

Jayewardene, C H S 1927-
   The penalty of death.

   Bibliography: p. 107
   Includes index.
   1. Capital punishment—Canada. 2. Murder—Canada.
   I. Title.
HV8699.C2J38   364.6'6'0971   77-167
ISBN 0-669-01464-8

Published simultaneously in Canada

Printed in the United States of America

International Standard Book Number: 0-669-01464-8

Library of Congress Catalog Card Number: 77-167

To my parents
who taught me how to love life and yet not
fear death.

Contents

List of Tables

Foreword

The question of whether a state should or should not include the penalty of death among its punishments for crime has been debated since ancient times. With the passage of centuries, the arguments pro and con have become traditional, but they seem to have concentrated on the problem of deterrence. Supporters of the penalty claim that it keeps in check or reduces the criminality it is designed to prevent; opponents deny the validity of that claim. The earliest record of that denial that I have found is in Thucydides' *History of the Peloponnesian War.*

The Mitylenians on the island of Lesbos had revolted against Athenian rule in 428 B.C. The revolt was finally suppressed the following year, and the Athenian Assembly decided to punish the rebels by exterminating them, thereby deterring other communities from revolting. The decision was rescinded, however, after the Assembly had listened to those opposing this policy. Cleon, the most powerful man in Athens, had urged his countrymen "to punish them (i.e. the rebels) as they deserve and teach your allies by a striking example that the penalty of rebellion is death. Let them once understand this and you will not have so often to neglect your enemies while you are fighting with your own confederates."

The reply to this argument was made by Diodotus in a lengthy oration, from which the following extracts have been culled. "The question before us as sensible men," he said, "is not their guilt but our interests. Though I prove them ever so guilty, I shall not, therefore, advise their death, unless it be expedient; nor though they should have claims to indulgence shall I recommend it, unless it be clearly for the good of the country. I consider that we are deliberating for the future more than for the present, and where Cleon is so positive as to the useful deterrent effects that will follow from making rebellion capital, I . . . as positively maintain the contrary. . . . Communities have enacted the penalty of death for many offenses far lighter than this; still hope leads men to venture, and no one ever yet put himself in peril without the inward conviction that he would succeed in his design. . . . All, states and individuals, are alike prone to err, and there is no law that will prevent them, or why should men have exhausted the list of punishments in search of enactments to protect them from evildoers? It is probable that in early times the penalties for the greatest offenses were less severe, and that as they were disregarded, the penalty of death has been by degrees in most cases arrived at, which is itself disregarded in like manner. Either then some means of terror more terrible than this must be discovered, or it must be owned that this restraint is useless; and that as long as poverty gives men the courage of necessity, or plenty fills them with the ambition which belongs to insolence and pride, and the other conditions of life remain each under the thraldom of some fatal and master passion, so long will the impulse never be wanting to drive men into danger. Hope also and cupidity, the one leading and the other following, the one conceiving the attempt, the other suggesting the facility of succeeding, cause the widest ruin, and, although invisible agents, are far stronger than the dangers that are seen. Fortune, too, powerfully helps the delusion, and by the unexpected aid that she sometimes lends, tempts men to venture with inferior means. . . . In fine, it is impossible to prevent, and only great simplicity can hope to prevent, human nature doing what it has once set its mind upon, by force of law or by any other deterrent force whatever."

Two and a half millennia have passed since Cleon and Diodotus debated the deterrent efficacy of capital punishment. In the meanwhile, and especially during the last two centuries, serious students of the problem have attempted, in numerous researches, to establish the truth or falsity of Cleon's belief. Dr. Jayewardene's book is a fine example of this quest.

Thorsten Sellin
Professor-Emeritus
Department of Sociology
University of Pennsylvania

Preface

Decision making where social policy is concerned is no easy task. What is best for society is not only a seemingly unanswerable question, it is also a question we apparently do not know how to answer. There are some who believe that social choice is essentially a function of individual preferences, and what is good for society is what the majority desire. There are others who feel that society is an entity distinct from and independent of the individuals who comprise it, and, what is good for society is unrelated to the needs and desires of the individual. Adherents of the former school of thought contend that social policy should be dependent on public opinion, frequently interpreted as some form of algebraic summation of individual sentiments. Proponents of the latter school claim that it should rest on a factual evaluation of what appears to be an inevitable cause-effect nexus. In the modern world of science and technology, there is a strong belief that the actions of rational humans should have their roots in fact rather than feeling. Hence—though emotions may predominate when decisions are made—discussions before and justifications after, see the predominance of rational and utilitarian arguments.

The objective evaluation of any social policy is contingent on its implementation. This does not necessarily mean that once a social policy has been implemented a definitive answer about its propriety could be given. It does, however, mean that until and unless the policy has been implemented, no scientific evaluation is possible. The existence of an opportunity for scientific evaluation does not always result in such evaluation. Both proponents and antagonists are rather loathe to embark on such a course of action, perhaps through fear that the rational and utilitarian arguments they used would be found to be without empirical support. The emotions that really compelled people to be committed to the one side or the other would then be bared and their rationality shown to be only a facade.

In the sphere of criminal justice, a question of relative importance has been the propriety of capital punishment. The literature on the subject is voluminous. As Sellin has pointed out, the arguments that have been used fall into two broad categories—emotional, which could not be subjected to empirical testing, and utilitarian, which could. Legislative changes involving capital punishment in many countries have afforded opportunities for empirical verification of the utilitarian arguments; and studies, capitalizing on these opportunities, indicate that the threat of capital punishment has no influence on the incidence of capital offences. Although the trend is for a decreasing use of capital punishment, by a total or partial abolition of it or a suspension of its imposition or infliction, there is a segment of the population in every country that sincerely believes capital punishment does serve a useful purpose and an equally potent segment that believes it does not. This division of the population results in periodic clamours for the reinstitution of the punishment in countries that have abolished it and for the abolition in countries that retain it.

Beliefs of people, on which social policy, social systems, and social structures are based, may not always be supported by fact. Some people are uncomfortable when a disjuncture occurs between what they believe things to be and what they really are. Others experience no such discomfort. Those who experience discomfort are forced to change their beliefs and demand social changes so that fact rather than fiction may govern our lives. But what is fact and what is fiction is not easy to discern. The scientist attempts to differentiate between the two through experimentation — a technique that is denied the social scientist by the very nature of the problems that are of interest. Changes in social policy, social structures, and social systems constitute a social experiment, which differs from the scientific experiment in that it lacks the careful planning that is associated with a scientific experiment and the manipulability of the variables involved. The social experiment offers the social scientist an experimental situation that affords the opportunity to evaluate resulting changes associated with the implemented with a cause-effect orientation. Though the social scientists' studies will never reveal the cause-effect relationship, they are the nearest they could get to it.

The five-year moratorium on capital punishment in Canada came to an end in December 1972. It was a social experiment, the evaluation of which was primarily the task of the legislators. Nonetheless, it provided the social scientist with an opportunity to attempt to answer questions connected with the subject. This book is the result of one such attempt. It, however, started as a purely personal quest for knowledge. Scientific curiosity dictated the analysis of murder statistics to ascertain the changes that occurred in the incidence and pattern of murder in Canada since the moratorium. This analysis resulted not in the better understanding of the problem but in a multitude of other questions that required answer. The result of the quest was a series of papers dealing with different aspects of the moratorium. Some of these papers have been published in scientific journals. Some have been read at meetings of scientific societies. They have all been brought together in this book with revisions and alterations to avoid repetition and overlap.

In the production of this book, the author has received assistance from many people. His wife, Dr. Hilda Jayewardene, and his mentor, Dr. Thorsten Sellin, read the manuscript at various stages of its development and benefitted the author with their criticisms and suggestions. His students, Mr. Avtar Singh and Mr. Lance Miron, assisted voluntarily in the collection of the data. His colleague, Dr. J. B. Garner, helped with the statistical analyses and his secretary, Miss Carol Herbert, patiently and painstakingly typed and retyped the manuscript. To all these persons, the author is deeply grateful.

C.H.S. Jayewardene
Department of Criminology
University of Ottawa
January 15, 1975

The Penalty of Death

1 The Moratorium on the Penalty of Death

A five-year moratorium on the penalty of death, except for the murder of a police officer or a prison official acting in the course of duty, came into effect on December 29, 1967. This moratorium could be looked on as the culmination of an abolitionist movement that originated in 1946. The movement apparently received its impetus from the proposal in the United Kingdom to abolish capital punishment for a trial period of five years. Although the history of the movement against capital punishment in Canada does not parallel that in the United Kingdom,[1] what happened there had an effect on what happened here, and when it was proposed to abolish capital punishment in the United Kingdom, it was thought that a similar move would be made in Canada. In preparation for this move the Financial Post[2] published the opinion of prominent Canadians on the question. The majority favoured the retention of the penalty. These people agreed that capital punishment was a relic of barbarism, but as murder itself was barbaric, they contended that death was a fitting punishment for it. They believed that the penalty of death was the most efficient deterrent against murder and felt conditions in Canada did not warrant a change. There were some who favoured abolition. They did so because they felt the penalty was no deterrent. An additional reason was their belief that the accused's life depended on the effectiveness of retained counsel and that jury verdicts tended to cancel legal considerations. They also thought that abolition was in keeping with life under the leadership of Christ. Few were neither against nor for abolition. They thought that Canada should await the results of the British experiment before making her move.

The first move in Parliament in this connection was made in 1948 when the then Minister of Justice, Hon. J. L. Ilsey, moved Bill No. 337, to amend the Criminal Code. One of the amendments dealt with the crime of infanticide — a new category of manslaughter — referring to those cases where an infant was killed by its mother while the balance of her mind was disturbed.[3] The amendment was considered an attempt to restrict the imposition of the penalty of death in spite of the fact that Mr. Ilsey stressed the government had no intention of changing the punishment for murder.

The real attempt to abolish the penalty of death came in 1950 in the form of Bill No. 2 "to amend the Criminal Code to abolish the penalty of death," moved by Mr. W. Ross Thatcher, member for Moose Jaw.[4] Being a private member's bill it was treated with the levity that private member's bills usually receive. It had its first reading on February 20, 1950. The second reading was

1

moved on April 20, 1950. It was debated for a few hours on June 6th and was
to be debated again for a few hours on June 20th. The bill was finally withdrawn
because Mr. Thatcher believed that it had not had the benefit of a full discussion
and the chances of it being accepted were poor.[5] The Bill, however, did serve a
purpose: it evoked a policy statement as to whether executions would be suspended till Parliament had completed its deliberations.[6] In 1953, Thatcher moved
a similar Bill.[7] This he did, he claimed, because he had received from the public,
since the last Bill, a spate of letters indicating a strong public unexpressed desire
to have the penalty of death abolished. This Bill too was withdrawn, but this
withdrawal was made on the suggestion of the Minister of Justice, Hon. Stuart S.
Garson, who pointed out that the matter was being dealt with by a special committee working to revise the existing criminal law and produce a consolidated
Criminal Code.

The special committee produced its revision but as far as capital punishment
was concerned, its recommendation was that the question should be studied by a
Royal Commission or a Joint Committee of the House and Senate. A similar
suggestion was made with respect to corporal punishment and lotteries. Conse-
quent to these recommendations, the House of Commons accepted the motion
of Justice Minister Garson to appoint a Joint Committee to study the three
topics. Unlike the Royal Commission of the United Kingdom, the work of the
committee was not to be restricted to the revision of the existing law: it could
investigate the feasibility of the abolition of capital punishment and make a
recommendation to that effect.[8] Most commissions on capital punishment, the
world over, have recommended abolition, although the recommendations have
seldom been acted on. The Joint Committee of the House and Senate was an
exception in this respect. It recommended the retention of capital punishment
as the mandatory punishment for murder, the retention of capital punishment
for treason and piracy, no change in the definition of murder, no degrees of
murder, no special provisions for women, the abolition of capital punishment
for offenders under eighteen years and its restricted use for offenders under
twenty-one, full disclosure of the Crown's case to the accused, provision of
competent counsel and assistance in producing evidence, mandatory plea of
nonguilty to capital offences, automatic appeal to the Provincial Court of
Appeal, appeal as a right of the convicted person to the Supreme Court of
Canada, centralized places of execution in each province, the abolition of hanging and its replacement with executions by the alternative of the gas chamber.[9]
These recommendations were made because of rejection of the main argument
against the penalty of death—that it does not possess any special deterrent
power—and the acceptance of other subsidiary ones—the execution of children,
errors of judgment leading to the execution of the innocent, the inability of
poor people to obtain the full benefits of the system, the brutality of hanging
as a form of punishment, and the cost involved in erecting a scaffold in each
and every prison on the rare occasion of an execution there.

The Joint Committee completed its work in 1956, and in the intervening period there was a lull in the movement against the penalty except for a move to stop executions until the study was completed. The move, of course, was not successful. In accordance with the earlier established policy[10] it was contended that it was unwise, by executive action, to bring about in effect a change in law that only Parliament could lawfully make.[11] Yet, the Royal Prerogative of Mercy was used with increasing generosity resulting in a decreasing number of executions and several questions on commutation asked in Parliament.[12]

With the publication of the Report of the Joint Committee, bills to amend the Criminal Code and abolish the penalty of death were introduced. On December 9, 1957, Harold E. Winch, Member for Vancouver East, moved for leave to introduce Bill No. 239 "to amend the Criminal Code restricting capital punishment to certain offences."[13] The bill, however, was not debated. A similar bill was introduced by Mr. Winch the next year. This bill was debated but adjourned without a vote being taken.[14] In the following year too the drama was repeated. The bill was introduced and debated but the debate was not permitted to proceed to its logical conclusion.[15] This bill was introduced by Frank McGee, Member for York-Scarborough, who was responsible for the introduction, in the next year, of a similar bill (No. C-6) that suffered a similar fate.[16] By now the question of the penalty of death had become more than an idiosyncratic pastime of a few Parliamentarians, and bills seeking to abolish it were being taken more seriously. Attempts were made by Parliamentarians to get the government to give these bills serious consideration[17] and when the government decided that it would not allow time for the conclusion of the debate on Bill No. C6 introduced by a private member, it was constantly reminded of this fact with a demand for its continuation and conclusion[18] and goaded into introducing its own legislation on the subject.[19]

When the next session of Parliament opened it was announced in the Speech from the Throne that "amendments will be proposed to the Criminal Code having to do with capital punishment."[20] But it was only five months later that the bill was debated.[21] The bill, No. C-92, was designed to permit the classification of murder, for which the mandatory punishment was death, into capital murder carrying the mandatory punishment of death, and noncapital murder carrying the mandatory punishment of life imprisonment. The basis of the classification was to be the quantum of deliberation and planning that preceded the act. Those cases that were not characterized by deliberation and planning were to be labelled noncapital as it was felt that in these cases the imposition or execution of the death penalty ought not to be provided. The purpose of the bill, as stated by Justice Minister E. D. Fulton, was "to bring the present position with regard to capital punishment into line with present-day ideas on crime and punishment." It was not, Mr. Fulton declared, "an abolitionist measure or a first step towards abolition." The bill itself was not hailed as a progressive measure but it was carried—139 voting for it and 21 against—though not without the usual moves to delay its passage with motions for referral to special committees. After its passage through Parliament, certain questions about the wording of the bill were raised, and the bill was referred to the Standing Committee on Banking and Commerce. At this Committee, Justice Minister Fulton pointed out that the questions resulted from a belief that the government intended restricting the infliction of capital punishment more than what it actually intended to and had inadvertently failed to do so in the legislation.[22] The passage of the bill, however, did not cry a halt to the abolitionist movement. At the next session of Parliament private members asked for an opportunity to review capital punishment,[23] introduced bills "to amend the Criminal Code to abolish capital punishment except for treason"[24] and asked questions regarding methods of execution[25] and the number of persons awaiting death.[26]

The general election of 1963 saw a change in political power. The Liberals were handed the reins of government. Though it was members of this party that were trying to goad the earlier government to abolish the death penalty, when the twenty-sixth Parliament assembled, the Liberals had abolition as neither government nor party policy. The only reference to capital punishment during the first session of that Parliament was a private member's bill on the order paper: "Bill C.37, to amend the Criminal Code and abolish capital punishment except for treason."[27] During the second session of that Parliament a similar bill—Bill C.12—was on the order paper again. This bill was debated on March 24, 1964, but was adjourned without the question coming to a vote[28] and with the government displaying no desire to have the vote.[29] Yet in 1963 and in 1964 no one was executed: all sentences of death were commuted to life imprisonment with the exercise of the Royal Prerogative of Mercy. The government reluctance to permit the bill to be fully debated, was consequently interpreted as an expression not of the nonpartisan nature of the subject but of the strategy of a proabolitionist government—de jure retention with de facto abolition—an interpretation that provoked a number of questions on the subject.[30]

In the Throne Speech opening the third session of the twenty-sixth Parliament, the government declared its intention of affording the House an opportunity to decide the issue of capital punishment.[31] Insisting, however, on the nonpartisan nature of the subject, Minister of Justice Guy Favreau announced, during the debate on the address in response to the Speech from the Throne, that he had ordered officials of the Department of Justice to prepare a comprehensive white paper on capital punishment that would be available to Members of the House before the question was debated. He also announced the government's intention to permit a free vote because of the emotions that would be involved.[32] In the meantime the government continued its generous exercise of the Royal Prerogative of Mercy, and questions on the subject, designed to embarrass the government, continued to be asked.[33]

At the first session of the twenty-seventh Parliament a bill to abolish capital punishment presented by a private member was debated. During this session of Parliament there were, on the order paper, four bills seeking to amend the Criminal Code to abolish capital punishment. The bill debated represented all of them.[34] Although the bill was a private member's, reflecting neither government nor party policy, there was sufficient indication that it did have the sympathetic support of the government. The Speech from the Throne at the opening of the twenty-seventh Parliament promised the House that it would be given an opportunity to discuss the issue of capital punishment,[35] and the debate on the address in response to the Speech from the Throne saw many expressions of hope that the penalty of death would be abolished.[36] These hopes, however, were not to be fulfilled for, after a protracted debate, the House rejected the motion, 112 voting for it and 143 against.[37]

On November 9, 1967, Solicitor-General L. T. Pennell moved the second reading of Bill No. C-168 "to amend the Criminal Code respecting death sentence and life imprisonment."[38] During the debate in 1966, three amendments, all of which were defeated, were proposed. The amendments sought to limit the abolition, first to certain forms of murder—retaining it for the murder of peace officers acting in the course of duty—and second to an experimental period of five years. Bill No. C-168, introduced by Solicitor-General Pennell, partly as a result of pressures from Members of the House to do so,[39] sought, as he pointed out, to retain the penalty of death for the murder of a peace officer—police, prison, parole, and probation officers—and to limit the abolition for a trial period of five years. These two provisions removed from the bill the objections voiced by a number of Parliamentarians in the earlier debate, and in doing so, maximized the likelihood that the bill would have a successful passage through the House. In moving the second reading of the bill, Mr. Pennell stressed that he did so through a deep conviction that capital punishment was wrong, and, appreciating that others may have equally strong views differing from him, declared the government's intention to permit a free vote on it. The passage of the bill was by no means easy. Several moves were made to adjourn the debate and to refer it to committees, both special and of the whole House, for more intense study of the question before it was finally answered. The moves, however, were defeated and the bill passed 114 voting for and 87 against.[40]

The moratorium on the penalty of death has been attributed to an ideological commitment of the Liberal Party to abolition. Though both the Conservative Government's bill of 1961 and the Liberal Government's bill of 1967 were designed to redefine murder and limit the imposition and execution of the penalty of death, the former bill is looked on as a retentionist and the latter an abolitionist, mainly because the limitation of the imposition of the penalty was slight in the earlier and extensive in the later. When to this is added Attorney General Fulton's emphatic claim that the bill he introduced was not an abolitionist move nor even a first step toward abolition and Solicitor General Pennell's contention that he moved the bill with a deep sense of conviction that capital punishment was wrong, it is not difficult to see how the Conservative Party becomes associated with an ideological commitment to retention and the Liberal Party an ideological commitment to abolition. Yet if the historical events are reviewed in their correct perspective both parties are found to have been reluctant to introduce any legislation that would alter the status quo. Both parties, when in power, displayed a profound contempt for the private member's bills seeking to amend the Criminal Code and abolish capital punishment. Both parties sought to produce the change by executive rather than legislative action. Both parties were goaded into moving the bills that they finally introduced. That the one is now viewed as a retentionist and the other as abolitionist does not appear to be because of their ideological commitment but because of the result of the circumstances in which they were situated. It was the Liberal Government's legislation that limited the imposition of the penalty of death to almost the point of abolition, but then the legislation which the Conservative Governments had been earlier forced to introduce left the Liberal Government no choice in the further legislation that they were then forced to introduce. It was the Liberal Government that commuted every sentence of death, but the pattern of commutation set by previous Conservative Governments left them no choice.[41] It was as if destiny was unfolding itself unobtrusively so as to make the change that was occurring appear congruous with the will of the people.

Whatever the ideological commitments of political parties may be, the moratorium settled, at least for a period of time, a question that was becoming highly controversial and political. It was the compromise between the strong retentionist and abolitionist emotions. It ensured the retentionists that the question would be asked once again and at the same time it ensured the abolitionists that the question would be asked again only after a period of time. In as much as the execution of a child or woman, the revelation of the execution of an innocent man, or the technical bungling of execution emphasizing its brutality adds to the momentum of an abolitionist movement, when the penalty of death has been abolished, there is a possibility of rescission of the abolition act because of a particularly outrageous murder, as happened in Ceylon.[42] This the moratorium prevents.[43] For the advantage that the moratorium confers, it imposes a disadvantage. It places the responsibility on ensuring the change on those who were responsible for initially securing it. A moratorium is designed to establish empirically the beneficial nature of a social measure that has no ideological consensus. It is essentially an experiment in social defense.

Notes

1. E. A. Tuttle (1961) *The Crusade Against Capital Punishment* (London: Stevens and Stevens).

2. *Financial Post* (1964) October 12th.

3. Canada (1948) *Debates: House of Commons* 20th Parliament, 4th Session. 5184-5188.

4. Canada (1950) *Debates: House of Commons* 21st Parliament, 2nd Session. 37.

5. Canada (1950) *Debates: House of Commons.* 2088, 3277-3283, 3890.

6. Canada (1950) *Debates: House of Commons.* 250.

7. Canada (1953) *Debates: House of Commons* 21st Parliament, 7th Session. 2259-2267, 4044-4049.

8. Canada (1953) *Debates: House of Commons* 22nd Parliament, 1st Session. 939-958, 1023-1036, 1047-1061.

9. Joint Committee of the Senate and the House of Commons on Capital Punishment, Corporal Punishment and Lotteries (1955) *Minutes of Proceedings and Evidence. Witness: J. Alex Edmison* (Ottawa: Queen's Printer).

10. Canada (1950) *Debates: House of Commons.* 250.

11. Canada (1954) *Debates: House of Commons* 22nd Parliament, 1st Session. 2652.

12. Canada (1957) *Debates: House of Commons* 23rd Parliament. 496, Canada (1960) *Debates: House of Commons* 24th Parliament, 3rd Session. 1885; Canada (1961) *Debates: House of Commons* 24th Parliament, 4th Session. 3829.

13. Canada (1957) *Debates: House of Commons.* 2567.

14. Canada (1958) *Debates: House of Commons* 24th Parliament, 2nd Session. 711-718, 2977-2983.

15. Canada (1959) *Debates: House of Commons* 24th Parliament, 2nd Session. 141-142, 2198-2204, 4960-4965.

16. Canada (1960) *Debates: House of Commons.* 1187-1223, 1441-1474.

17. Canada (1960) *Debates: House of Commons.* 39, 492-493.

18. Canada (1960) *Debates: House of Commons.* 1186-1187, 1435-1436, 2012-2021, 2252, 4767, 4988-4879, 6410, 7192-7193, 7324-7325, 7529-7533.

19. Canada (1960) *Debates: House of Commons.* 1646-1647, 2252-2253.

20. Canada (1960) *Debates: House of Commons.* 2-3.

21. Canada (1961) *Debates: House of Commons.* 5220-5248, 5299-5326, 5506-5565, 5879-5915.

22. Canada (1961) *Proceedings of the Standing Committee on Banking and Commerce to whom was referred the Bill C-92 entitled: An Act to Amend the Criminal Code (Capital Murder) 27.6.61* (Ottawa: Queen's Printer).

23. Canada (1962) *Debates: House of Commons* 25th Parliament, 1st Session. 2487.

24. Canada (1962) *Debates: House of Commons.* 375.

25. Canada (1962) *Debates: House of Commons.* 2812; Canada (1963) *Debates: House of Commons* 25th Parliament, 1st Session. 3382.

26. Canada (1963) *Debates: House of Commons.* 3386-3387.

27. Canada (1963) *Debates: House of Commons* 26th Parliament, 1st Session. 375.

28. Canada (1964) *Debates: House of Commons* 26th Parliament, 2nd Session. 1418-1426.

29. Canada (1964) *Debates: House of Commons.* 4930, 5205.

30. Canada (1965) *Debates: House of Commons* 26th Parliament, 2nd Session. 11469, 11628, 12878.

31. Canada (1965) *Debates: House of Commons* 26th Parliament, 3rd Session. 1-3.

32. Canada (1965) *Debates: House of Commons* 26th Parliament, 3rd Session. 4-10, 19-58, 64-89, 101-160, 172-207, 217-289, 309-335, 338-383.

33. Canada (1965) *Debates: House of Commons* 26th Parliament, 3rd Session. 982, 1450-1451, 2322, 2417, 2495, 3063-3064.

34. Canada (1966) *Debates: House of Commons* 27th Parliament, 1st Session. 5158-5159.

35. Canada (1966) *Debates: House of Commons.* 7-10.

36. Canada (1966) *Debates: House of Commons.* 28-83, 92-135, 152-205, 214-272, 282-305.

37. Canada (1966) *Debates: House of Commons.* 3067-3085, 3095, 3158, 3262, 3324, 3789-3852, 3865-3911.

38. Canada (1967) *Debates: House of Commons* 27th Parliament, 2nd Session. 4077, 4098, 4102-4118, 4142-4164, 4244-4266, 4274-4293, 4311-4320, 4336-4357, 4365-4381, 4570-4585, 4604-4621, 4629-4644, 4846-4861, 4879-4893.

39. Canada (1966) *Debates: House of Commons.* 6752, 8193, 8605, 10587.

40. Canada (1967) *Debates: House of Commons.* 4077, 4098, 4102-4118, 4142-4164, 4244-4266, 4274-4293, 4311-4320, 4336-4357, 4365-4381, 4570-4585, 4604-4621, 4629-4644, 4846-4861, 4879-4893.

41. C. H. S. Jayewardene (1972) "The Canadian Movement against the Penalty of Death." *Canad. Jour. Criminol. Correct.,* 14, 366-381.

42. C. H. S. Jayewardene (1961) "The Death Penalty in Ceylon." *Ceylon Journal of Historical and Social Studies,* 3, 166-186.

43. A. Normandeau (1964) "La Peine de Mort au Canada." *Rev. Droit pen. Criminol.,* 46, 547-559.

2   Deterrence and the Death Penalty

The propriety of capital punishment revolves round its deterrent power.[1] Rates of capital offences in retentionist and abolitionist states—and, in the same state, before and after abolition—have been compared to assess this deterrent power.[2] These studies have as their basis the logic succinctly stated by Mr. Silverman in the debate on capital punishment in the British House of Commons in 1964: "The only point about deterrence, and I think, the only rational ground on which a death penalty could ever be defended is that there are fewer murders if we have the death penalty than if we do not . . . "[3] Most studies have considered the total picture in a country, with the implication that the deterrent power of the penalty is uninfluenced by the character of either the offender or the victim. In the debate on capital punishment in Canada, however, the Canadian Association of Police Chiefs have contended that the abolition increases disproportionately the risk that police and other law enforcement officers must run.[4] Studies have hence been undertaken to ascertain what increase there is, if any, in the homicide of law enforcement officers[5] and of prison staff[6] following the abolition or suspension of the death penalty. Still other studies have sought to assess the influence that an actual execution has on homicide in the belief that the deterrent effect of the penalty would be more pronounced with the knowledge of its actual imposition than just its existence as a mere threat.[7] All these studies have led to the conclusion that the threat of the punishment does not have a perceptible effect on the incidence of homicide.[8] Yet, these findings have not been accepted as conclusive.

The reluctance to accept the findings of these studies as answering the crucial question of deterrence, however, has not been totally irrational. Part of the reluctance lies in the fact that though the studies are designed to specifically answer the question with the simple "more without, less with" formula, the negative answer that is offered does not result from its application. All studies do not show that there has been no increase in the incidence with the abolition. Some show an increase, some a decrease. These inconsistent results have been interpreted as a demonstration that the incidence of homicide is dependent not on the threatened punishment but on a multitude of other factors, and from this interpretation the conclusion that the death penalty does not exert a deterrent effect has been inferred. Part of the reluctance lies in the intuitive feeling that the simple "more without, less with" formula fails to take into account a number of significant factors, and, in doing so, tests not the deterrent effect of the punishment but something else. Zimring,[9] for example, contends

9

that the before-after and abolitionist-retentionist comparisons are really not the
with-without comparisons it is claimed they are. Abolition does not result in
the legalization of the act. There is always some other punishment threatened
so that what is being tested is, at the most, the marginal deterrent effect of the
penalty of death. Even this position appears untenable unless the comparison
is with data relating to those offences that carry these punishments as mandatory ones. When all homicides are utilized in the tests, the comparison is
essentially that of situations where the same punishments are differentially
inflicted.

As deterrence carries the connotation of prevention, the deterrent effect of
capital punishment is best evaluated in terms of the number of persons prevented
from committing homicide by the penalty. The apparent unanswerability of this
question stems from the assumed universal applicability of the hedonistic philosophy coupled with a teleological interpretation of human behaviour that
endows the human with complete freedom of will, that permits the expression
of any form of behaviour at any time, no matter what the circumstances may
be. Even the view that homicide is a teleological act does not make it solely
dependent on the whims and fancies of the individual. To commit homicide the
individuals must have not only the intention and capacity to do so, they must
also be placed in a situation in which they are likely to do so.[10] Punishment
can have a deterrent effect by influencing the individual's freedom of will only
in a situation in which the outlawed behaviour presents itself as a possible reaction. Those who are not in this situation cannot be deterred by the punishment, because the outlawed behaviour does not enter into the considerations.
If it is the only possible reaction, the threatened punishment again exercises no
deterrence. The concept of free will does not abnegate the possibility of the
individual being placed in a situation in which he or she has no decision to make.
She or he could be in such a situation by the previous exercise of free will—an
exercise that rendered it no longer exerciseable.

The more sophisticated before-after and abolitionist-retentionist comparison
studies conceded the existence of two sets of factors influencing the incidence
of homicide. These two factors could be labelled the social conditions factor
and the punishment factor. The influence of the latter is sought to be studied
through comparison of the incidence of homicide under variation of the punishment with the social conditions factor maintained constant. This latter
objective, essential for evaluation, is thought achievable if the comparison is
limited to periods where there was no apparent differences in social conditions.[11]
The dynamic nature of society, however, belies this assumption. What the
studies seek to do can only be done when the comparison is of the incidence
of homicide in the same country at the same time with the penalty of death
in force and with it nonoperant—a comparison that is a physical impossibility.

The deterrent effect of a penalty comprises essentially two components:
the prevention of the commission of a crime by those who have already

committed it once; and the prevention of the commission of a crime by those who have not committed it before. These two components have been described by Andenaes[12] as comprising two independent forces labelled by him as the specific deterrent effect and the general deterrent effect respectively. The division is of significance when the death penalty is considered as the imposition of the penalty removes offenders permanently from society and prevents them from making any further contribution to the problem. The specific deterrent effect of capital punishment is 100 percent in as much as it successfully deters those on whom it has been inflicted from ever repeating their act. Consequently theoretically at least, one of the effects of the abolition of the penalty of death, is to reduce the specific deterrent effect of the punishment by making offenders available for the commission of a second offence. The theoretical position, however, assumes a factual basis only under certain conditions. If homicide offenders, as is widely believed, rarely recidivate,[13] nonexecution of homicide offenders does not alter the specific deterrent effect of the punishment, for what the abolition does then is to save not potential recidivists but nonrecidivists.

Studies in homicide recidivism, however, indicate that the widely held view is far from factual. Anttila and Westling[14] studied the risk involved in releasing persons convicted of criminal homicide. They studied persons sentenced to life imprisonment during the period of January 1, 1929 through December 31, 1958 in Finland. There were 542 such persons, of whom 340 had been released and were living in freedom at the time of study. After release 10 had committed a new homicide in a total of 4324.5 man years in freedom giving a risk of recidivism to a homicide offender of 0.23 percent. Studies of capital offenders released on parole in 22 states of the United States has revealed them to be more or less ideal parolees with only 11 of 197 violating parole with a new offence.[15] A similar situation has been found to exist in the State of California during the period 1945 through 1954. By 1956, only 9 of 342 convicted for first degree murder paroled during this period had committed a felony and of these only one a second homicide.[16] In New York 63 persons convicted of first degree murder during the period of July 1, 1930 through December 31, 1961 were released on parole—none committed a second homicide during parole. From January 1945 through December 1961, 514 persons convicted for second degree murder were paroled. Only two committed a second homicide—one less than a month after release and the other a little over a year.[17] In Ohio, not one of 273 first degree murderers paroled 1945-1965 committed a second homicide.[18] In Pennsylvania 0.4 percent of criminal homicide parolees committed a homicide during their first year on parole.[19] In England and Wales, 156 persons convicted of murder were released during the period 1934-1948 and only one was reconvicted of murder: in Scotland 9 prisoners convicted of murder were discharged during 1931-1949, none were reconvicted of murder.[20] In Canada the situation does not appear to be any different. Between 1959 and 1967, thirty-two commuted violent offenders were released on parole. By the end of 1967, only one had been convicted of a further offence, which did not involve further loss of life. From 1920-1967, 119 first degree murderers serving sentences of life imprisonment (a commutation of the death sentence) were released on parole. Only one offender had killed a second time.[21]

All these studies emphasize the low probability of a capital offender committing a second capital offence, promoting the image of a capital offender as a relatively innocuous individual. But before we accept this interpretation as valid, it behooves us to explore the possibility of other interpretations especially when they are used as arguments in the debate. The only attempt made to quantitatively assess the probability that a homicide offender will commit a second homicide has been made by Anttila and Westling.[22] The probability they found (0.23 percent) means that a homicide offender once released from prison has a likelihood of committing a second homicide of 0.0023 in any one year. In absolute terms, this likelihood is low. The study has been conducted in Finland, where the average annual homicide rate of about 3.5 per 100,000 makes the country one with neither an excessively high rate nor an extraordinarily low one.[23] With such a rate the probability that any citizen would commit a homicide in any one year is 0.000035 making the probability of a released homicide offender committing a homicide in any one year relatively high. The homicide rate, however, based on the total population and taking into consideration a multitude of people physically incapable of committing homicide does not give us a reasonable assessment of the probability of an individual committing homicide.[24] As the group most likely to commit homicide in a country are young adult males[25] a more comparable comparison of the probability of committing homicide as a first offender and a recidivist would involve the homicide rates specific to this group. In Finland the homicide rates specific to males aged 25-44 years old and 45-64 years old is 5.6 per 100,000.[26] These figures make the homicide offender over 41 times as likely to commit his second homicide as is a young adult male to commit his first. The impact on the actual incidence of homicide is, however, not as great as the statement is meaningful only when applied to a group. The contribution that homicide offenders saved from death by the abolition of the death penalty would make to the homicide problem by a second homicide depends on the number that are to be saved because of the abolition.

All homicide offenders are not executed; some are not apprehended, some are apprehended but not prosecuted, some are prosecuted but not convicted, some are convicted but not sentenced to death, and then some are sentenced to death but not executed. A survey of 146 countries (replies received from 128) revealed that while only 18 countries had removed the penalty from their statutes, 36 never used the penalty, and 13 retained it as a penalty for only unusual crimes. What is even more surprising was that the average number of executions per annum in countries retaining and using the penalty was fantastically low. The average number was 0.1-1.0 in five countries, 1.1-5.0 in twenty-four, 5.1-10.0 in three, 10.1-25.0 in five, 25.1-50.0 in two, and 50.1-100.0 in only one.[27] In England and Wales, there were 7454 murders during the 50-year period 1900-1949 but only 520 executions during the same period.[28] In Canada during the period 1950 through 1964, only 77 persons were executed although 262 persons were sentenced to death.[29]

What the abolition of the penalty of death does to the homicide problem as far as recidivism is concerned is to add the recidivist contribution of those who would have been executed. Adverting to the Canadian situation, had the 77 persons executed during the period 1950 through 1964 not been executed but released into society immediately, they would have increased the homicides by 2 during the 15 year period, on the basis that a homicide offender is 41 times as likely to commit a second homicide as is a young adult to commit a first. If all sentenced to death were executed, the execution of 262 prisoners during the 15 year period could conceivably have reduced the total number of homicides during this period by 6. These figures are pertinent in considering yet another argument for the penalty of death. Barzun[30] contends "the uncontrollable brute whom I want to put away is not to be punished for his misdeeds, nor used as an example or a warning: he is to be killed for the protection of others, like the wolf that escaped not long ago in a Connecticut suburb."

As far as the specific deterrent effect of the death penalty is concerned, there are two other factors that have to be taken into consideration. The recidivist contribution to the homicide problem comprises four components—that of nonapprehended offenders, that of institutionalized offenders, that of offenders released to society after punishment, and that of executed offenders. The actual contribution depends on the proportion of homicide offenders in each of these groups and the probability that an offender in each category would commit the second homicide. The specific deterrent effect, hence, can be assessed only by determination of the change in the proportions of the offenders in each group attributable to the abolition of the death penalty.

If homicide offenders released from prison are capable of committing a second offence, there is no reason to believe that nonapprehended and institutionalized offenders are unlikely to do so. Homicide offenders are generally conceived of as being first time offenders, and the homicide is conceived of as the solitary blot on an unblemished character.[31] But the empirical evidence does not support this hypothesis. Of the nonapprehended homicide offenders who stood in the docks of the Assize Courts of England and Wales in the period March 21, 1957 through December 31, 1962, there were several who had committed or attempted to commit a previous homicide.[32] Shaw[33] gives a number of examples of persons who committed several homicides before they were finally apprehended. Anttila and Westling[34] in their study of 542 homicide offenders sentenced to life imprisonment in Finland during the period 1929 through 1958, found 20 to have committed a previous homicide. Jayewardene and Ranasinghe[35] in a study of 88 homicides committed in the Southern

Province of Ceylon in 1960, found one of 194 suspects with a previous conviction for attempted homicide, though none with even a suspicion of having committed a previous homicide. The F.B.I. Careers in Crime file data on 194,550 offenders arrested during the period 1963 through 1967 show that 89.2 percent of the 2013 persons arrested for criminal homicide had never been arrested before, 10.0 percent had one arrest while 0.8 percent had two or more arrests for major crimes. The data also reveal that 15.4 percent of second arrest offenders arrested for criminal homicide had been arrested on the first occasion too for criminal homicide and 16.3 percent of third arrest offenders arrested for criminal homicide had had their second arrest for criminal homicide as well: 6.7 percent of all criminal homicide offenders had a previous conviction.[36]

In prison, too, homicide offenders are known to have committed a second homicide. Data obtained from seven penal institutions in the United States for the decade 1949-1958 revealed that of a total of twelve homicides committed in these institutions four were committed by homicide offenders.[37] Sellin[38] obtaining data from federal and state institutions in the United States found twenty-six homicides committed in 1964 in a total of fourteen institutions. Of these, five were committed by homicide offenders—two serving life sentences for capital murder, two long-term sentences for noncapital murder, and one for manslaughter. Two other homicides were committed by armed robbers—one under a death sentence and one under a life sentence. In the Illinois State Prison at Joliet, there were only two homicides during the period July 1, 1956 through December 31, 1964.[39] In 1965 there were sixty-one homicides committed in penal institutions of the United States—nineteen of these were committed by persons serving sentences for one or another form of homicide.[40] Anttila, Törnudd, and Westling[41] found that ten of the males serving life sentences for homicide in Finland during 1929-1958 had committed a second homicide in prison. This they found was equivalent to a rate of 0.23 per 100 man years.

The computation of the probability of commission of a second homicide while serving a sentence in prison does not pose too difficult a task. Anttila and his coworkers[42] have done precisely this by relating the number of homicides committed by homicide offenders in prison to the number of man years spent by them in prison. The rate they obtained—0.23 per 100 man years—is no different to the homicide rate for homicide offenders after release.[43] The computation of the probability of commission of a second homicide by a homicide offender who has not been apprehended is more problematic. The size of this group of homicide offenders in society must be known, and the number of homicides committed by them must also be known. The work of Anttila and Westling[44] seems to suggest that they make a 3.7 percent contribution to the homicide problem—this was the proportion of homicide recidivists among the homicide offenders who were apprehended.

In Finland about 50 percent of the homicide cases results in a conviction

of the suspect[45] so that about 50 percent of the offenders remains unapprehended each year. With an annual average of about 100 homicides in a population of 3.5 million, the probability of an unapprehended homicide offender
committing a second homicide can be estimated at 0.3 percent. The Task
Force on Science and Technology to the President's Commission on Law Enforcement and Administration of Justice attempted to calculate the probability
that a person once arrested for murder and manslaughter would be arrested
again for the same offence. Using a simulated sample of 1000 offenders
arrested for the first time at age sixteen and rearrest patterns computed using
a rearrest matrix of probabilities calculated from the data published in the
Minnesota Board of Corrections document "Crime Revisited," 1965 Uniform
Crime Reports, and the 1965 Statistical Tables of the Federal Bureau of
Prisons, they found that the probability that a prisoner once arrested for murder
or nonnegligent manslaughter, if arrested again, would be arrested for murder or
nonnegligent manslaughter was 0.025. The simulation sample also revealed that
1000 persons arrested for murder and nonnegligent manslaughter would experience 40 rearrests for murder and nonnegligent manslaughter in their life time.[46]

The abolition of the death penalty converts the recidivist potential of a
certain proportion of homicide offenders from 0 to 0.23 percent and consequently increases the recidivist contribution to the problem. If, in addition,
the abolition of the penalty makes the solution of homicide cases and the
conviction of homicide offenders easier, the abolition of the penalty would
also decrease the recidivist potential of a certain proportion of homicide
offenders from 0.3 percent to 0.23 percent and consequently decrease the
recidivist contribution to the problem. The net effect—the algebraic sum of
these two opposing forces—represents the contribution made by the abolition
to the incidence of homicide, and hence the specific deterrent effect of the
penalty. With just a small proportion of homicide offenders executed, the
abolition of the penalty of death may tend to decrease rather than increase
the recidivist component of the problem.

Ascertainment of the deterrent effect of the penalty of death involves the
determination of the number of homicides prevented by the existence of the
penalty. In analyzing the deterrent effect in terms of (1) a general deterrence—
prevention of nonoffenders from committing a first offence—and (2) a specific
deterrence—prevention of offenders from recidivating—it is found that the
contribution made by the penalty of death to the homicide problem comprises three components. First, there are those who are deterred from committing their first offence. These are persons whose behaviour is fashioned
by punishment or its threat and who are in addition placed in a homicidogenic
situation. With the abolition of the death penalty it is reasonable to assume
that this contribution would increase. Since the contribution depends first
on the size of that segment of the population whose behaviour is fashioned
by punishment and second on the size of the section of this segment placed

in a homicidogenic situation, its actual magnitude would be dependent more on social factors than on the punishment component. Second, there are those who are executed and prevented from committing a second offence. With abolition this contribution is likely to increase. The magnitude of this contribution, of course, depends on the actual number of persons not executed as a result of abolition. Usually this is extremely small. A third contribution involves variations in apprehension, prosecution, and convictions of offenders. These variations effect the recidivist component. Usually it tends to decrease the number of homicides after abolition, but this need not be the invariable position. The number of homicides prevented by the death penalty can only be accurately assessed by the determination of the magnitude of these three component contributions. It cannot be done in holistic terms. The propriety of the death penalty, however, does not depend on the number of homicides that are prevented. Even with the deterrent effect maximal, all homicides cannot be prevented. The answer revolves round the pragmatic question of gain in terms of homicides prevented at cost in terms of homicide offenders executed. If a number of homicides are prevented by the execution of an equal number of homicide offenders what advantage in terms of human life accrues society? This, however, is a moral question answerable in accordance with the values cherished by society. In seeking the answer to this question it should perhaps be remembered that the abolition of the death penalty does not legalize the behaviour punished by it. Even after abolition, capital offences are illegal. They are punishable with some other penalty. The deterrent effect studied and the deterrent effect pertinent is not the total deterrent power of the penalty, but the marginal deterrent effect of the severer death penalty over the lesser substitute.[47]

Notes

1. Royal Commission on Capital Punishment (1954) *Evidence 30th Day Witness: Prof. Thorsten Sellin.* February 1, 1954 (London: H.M.S.O.).

2. Royal Commission on Capital Punishment (1954) *Report* (London: H.M.S.O.); K. F. Schuessler (1952) "The Deterrent Influence of the Death Penalty." *Ann. Amer. Acad. Pol. Soc. Sci.,* 284, 54-62; T. Sellin (1955) "Homicides in Retentionist and Abolitionist States." Appendix F. Joint Committee of the Senate and the House on Capital and Corporal Punishment and Lotteries. *Minutes of Proceedings and Evidence.* (Ottawa: Queen's Printer) 718-728; _____(1959) *The Death Penalty* (Philadelphia: American Law Institute); _____(1964) "Death and Imprisonment as Deterrents to Murder," in H.A. Bedeau, *The Death Penalty in America* (Garden City, N.Y.: Anchor-Doubleday) 274-284; G. B. Vold (1932) "Can the Death Penalty Prevent Crime." *Prison. Jour.,* October, 3-7.

3. House of Commons. Great Britain. (1964) *Parliamentary Debates* 704, 882.

4. G. Favreau (1965) *Capital Punishment* (Ottawa: Queen's Printer).

5. D. Campion (1955) "The State Police and the Death Penalty." Appendix F. Joint Committee of the Senate and House on Capital and Corporal Punishment and Lotteries. *Minutes of Proceedings and Evidence.* (Ottawa: Queen's Printer) 729-741; _____ (1964) "Does the Death Penalty Protect State Police?" in H. A. Bedeau, *The Death Penalty in America* (Garden City, N.Y.: Anchor-Doubleday) 314-315; Royal Commission on Capital Punishment (1954) *Evidence 30th Day*; T. Sellin (1967) "Death Penalty and Police Safety," in T. Sellin, *Capital Punishment* (New York: Harper and Row).

6. D. D. Akman (1966) "Homicides and Assaults in Canadian Penitentiaries." *Canad. Jour. Correc.*, 8, 284-299; _____ (1967) "Homicides and Assults in Canadian Penitentiaries." *Howard Jour. Penol.*, 12, 102-112; _____ (1967) "Homicides and Assaults in Canadian Penitentiaries" in T. Sellin, *Capital Punishment*, 161-168.

7. R. H. Dann (1935) "The Deterrent Effect of Capital Punishment" *Friends Social Service Series Bull.*, 29; L. D. Savitz (1958) "A Study of Capital Punishment." *Jour. Crim. Law Criminol.*, 48, 338-341; T. Sellin (1965) "The Inevitable End of Capital Punishment." *Crim. Law Quart.*, 8, 36-51.

8. Favreau, *Capital Punishment*. President's Commission on Law Enforcement and the Administration of Justice (1967) *The Challenge of Crime in a Free Society* (Washington, D.C.: Government Printing Office). United Nations (1965) *Capital Punishment* (New York: United Nations).

9. F. E. Zimring (1971) *Perspectives in Deterrence* (Washington, D.C.: Government Printing Office).

10. C. H. S. Jayewardene and H. Ranasinghe (1963) *Criminal Homicide in the Southern Province* (Colombo, Sri Lanka: Colombo Apothecaries Co. Ltd.).

11. Sellin "Homicides," 718-728.

12. J. Andenaes (1966) "The General Prevention Effects of Punishment." *Univ. Penns. Law Rev.*, 114, 949.

13. M. B. Clinard (1957) *The Sociology of Deviant Behaviour* (New York: Rinehart & Co. Ltd.). L. Lawes (1932) *Twenty Thousand Years in Sing Sing.* (New York: R. Long and R. R. Smith). T. Sellin (1964) "Capital Punishment" in D. Dressler, *Readings in Criminology and Penology* (New York: Columbia University Press). G B. Smith (1958) "Situational Murder Due to Emotional Stress." *Jour. Soc. Ther.*, 4, 173-181.

14. I. Anttila and A. Westling (1965) "The Pardoning of and Recidivism among Criminals Sentenced to Life Imprisonment." *Scand. Stud. Criminol.*, 1, 13-34.

15. G. I. Giardi and R. G. Farrow (1952) "The Paroling of Capital Offenders." *Ann. Amer. Acad. Pol. Soc. Sci.*, 284, 85-94.

16. Judiciary Committee (1957) *Report of the Subcommittee of the Judiciary Committee on Capital Punishment Pertaining to the Problems of the Death Penalty and its Administration in California.* Assembly Interim Committee Reports 1955-1957, Vol. 20, No. 3, Sacramento, p. 12.

17. J. M. Stanton (1969) "Murders on Parole." *Crime Delinq.*, 15, 149-155. State of New York. Executive Department (1964) *34th Annual Report of the Division of Parole for 1963* (Albany).

18. Ohio Adult Parole Authority (1966) *A Summary of Parole Performance of First Degree Murderers in Ohio for the Calendar Year 1965 and the Period 1945-1965* (Columbus).

19. Pennsylvania Board of Parole (1960) *A Comparison of Releases and Recidivists from June 1, 1946, to May 31, 1961* (Harrisburg).

20. Royal Commission on Capital Punishment (1954) *Report.*

21. C. Sheppard (1971) "Towards a Better Understanding of the Violent Offender." *Canad. Jour. Criminol. Corr.*, 13, 60-67.

22. Anttila and Westling "Pardoning of Recidivism," 1, 13-34.

23. C. H. S. Jayewardene (1964) "Criminal Homicide in Ceylon." *Prob. Child Care Jour.*, 3, 15-30.

24. C. H. S. Jayewardene (1969) "The Measurement of Criminal Homicide." *Prob. Child Care Jour.* 7, 1-4.

25. C. H. S. Jayewardene (1960) "Criminal Homicide. A Study in Culture Conflict." (Unpublished Ph.D. Dissertation. University of Pennsylvania).

26. United Nations (1957) *Demographic Year Book.* (New York: United Nations).

27. C. H. Patrick (1965) "The Status of Capital Punishment. A World Perspective." *Jour. Crim. Law Criminol.*, 55, 397-411.

28. Royal Commission on Capital Punishment (1954) *Report.*

29. Favreau, *Capital Punishment.*

30. J. Barzun (1962) "In Favor of Capital Punishment." *Amer. Schol.*, 31, 181-191. ____(1969) "In Favor of Capital Punishment. *Crime Delinq.*" 15, 21-28.

31. Clinard, *Sociology of Deviant Behavior.* Lawes, *Twenty Thousand Years.* Sellin (1964) "Capital Punishment."

32. T. Morris and L. Blom-Cooper (1964) *A Calendar of Murder* (London: Michel Joseph).

33. E. S. Shaw (1960) *A Companion to Murder* (London: Cassel).

34. Anttila and Westling, "Pardoning of Recidivism."

35. Jayewardene and Ranasinghe, *Criminal Homicide.*

36. D. J. Mulvihill, M. M. Tumin, and L. A. Curtiss (1969) *Crimes of Violence* (Washington, D.C.: Government Printing Office).

37. C. H. S. Jayewardene (1962) "Are Murderers Dangerous?" *Prob. Child Care Jour., 2*, 33-35.

38. T. Sellin (1965) "Homicides and Assaults in American Prisons." *Acta Criminol. Med. Leg. Jap., 31*, 1-4.

39. Sellin, "Homicides and Assaults," 31, 1-4.

40. T. Sellin (1967) "Prison Homicides," in T. Sellin: *Capital Punishment.* (New York: Harper and Row) 154-160.

41. I. Anttila, P. Törnudd, and A. Westling (1964) "Elinkautinen kuritushuonerangain Tus." *Kriminologinen Tutkimuslaitos,* 1-23.

42. Anttila, Tornudd, and Westling, "Elin Kautinen," 1-23.

43. Anttila and Westling, "Pardoning of Recidivism," 1, 13-34.

44. Anttila and Westling, "Pardoning of Recidivism," 1, 13-34.

45. C. H. S. Jayewardene "Criminal Homicide."

46. President's Commission on Law Enforcement and Administration of Justice (1967) *Task Force Report: Science and Technology* (Washington, D.C.: Government Printing Office).

47. F. E. Zimring (1971) *Perspectives on Deterrence* (Washington, D.C.: Government Printing Office).

3

Certainty and Severity for Deterrence

It is the assumption that pain and pleasure constitute the mainsprings of human action that endows punishment with a deterrent power. As people seek pleasure in preference to pain, the argument goes, the infliction of pain that tends to minimize the pleasure from an act tips the balance of probabilities against performance of that act in the conscious or unconscious deliberations governing the decision to act.[1] However, the empirical evidence for the deterrent efficacy of a punishment is frequently sought to be provided by the comparison of rates of crime under varying threats of punishment.[2] One method of empirically testing the deterrent effect of capital punishment has been to compare the rates of capital offences in abolitionist and retentionist countries or before and after the abolition of capital punishment in the same country.[3] This model assumes that the threat of punishment is no different from the imposition that the theoretical justification contends carries the deterrent power. Such an assumption is reasonable in view of the fact that one form of deterrence—the general deterrence[4]—that prevents the first offence is the threat. The imposition of the punishment acts as a second or specific deterrence[5] preventing the repetition of the act. However, even in the case of general deterrence, the potency of the threat lies not in the threat alone. If a threat is an empty one that cannot or will not ever be actualized, it will not influence the conscious or unconscious deliberations of the individual. The capacity of a threat to act as a deterrent, hence, is dependent on the certainty of its actualization.

An attempt to study the influence of this factor in the deterrent efficacy of the death penalty has been made by Schuessler.[6] He found a negative, although insignificant, correlation between the certainty of execution of the death penalty and the homicide rate, providing some evidence for the importance of certainty. More definitive evidence of its role comes from the study of parking violations in a midwestern university in the United States, where an increase in certainty and severity led to the reduction in violations.[7] Instances where police immobilization[8] and increased police surveillance,[9] varying the certainty of punishment, were associated with an increase or decrease in crime also exist to underscore the dependency of a threat on actual imposition for its deterrent power.

In the study of a deterrent effect of punishment, Gibbs[10] contends that a distinction should be made between the two aspects of a legal reaction—the normative or threatened punishment and the actual or inflicted punishment. In as much as the former becomes meaningful because of the latter, studies of the deterrent effect of the punishment should use as its independent variable not its normative but its actual aspect. The latter, he contends, comprise essentially two elements—severity and certainty—that could be measured as far as homicide was concerned in terms of the time served on a homicide sentence and the proportion of homicide offenders admitted to prison respectively. The relationship of these two elements to the average annual homicide rate will reveal the real deterrent efficacy of the punishment. Using data, subject to the usual deficiencies of published statistics, for the United States, he has demonstrated the influence of the two factors. The homicide rates are above the median in 80 percent of the eleven states where severity and certainty are low as compared with 9 percent of the eleven states that are high on both. Both severity and certainty of punishment bear an inverse relationship to the incidence of the offence, but, the statistical analysis indicates, the association is far greater for certainty.

A similar study has been made by Tittle[11] who—while accepting the Gibbs' definition of certainty as an estimate of the probability that a crime, come to the attention of the police, will eventuate in imprisonment, and of severity, as the length of time served by the prisoner—differed in the computation of the actual indices. Certainty was measured by Gibbs[12] by dividing the relevant number of persons admitted to prison in 1960 by the corresponding 1959-1960 average annual number of cases occurring in the state, and by Tittle[13] by dividing the number of admissions 1959-1963 by the crimes known to the police 1958-1962. Severity was measured by Gibbs by the median number of months served while the Tittle measure was the mean number of months served. A third difference lay in the deviance index. Gibbs used the average annual rate 1959-1961 while Tittle computed his index using the mean average number of crimes 1959-1963 and the 1960 population. Tittle found a negative correlation between certainty of punishment and the incidence of the offence, and, in the case of homicide—and homicide only—between severity and the incidence. This led him to the hypothesis that severity acts as a deterrence only when certainty is high, supporting Gibbs' supposition of an additive effect of certainty and severity.

A third and similar test of the deterrence hypothesis was made by Chiricos and Waldo[14] but with its extension first by examination of the relationship for three points in time and second by relating changes in the rates of crime to prior changes in the certainty and severity of punishment. They found little support for the hypothesis that crime rates and the severity and certainty of punishment are inversely related. They attribute the inconsistency of findings both in their study alone and between their study and the other studies to the unsuitability of the data for such analysis. In more recent times, the same model has been used by Teevan[15] to test the deterrent effects of punishment with Canadian data. Defining certainty operationally as the ratio of court convictions to the number of reported crimes, he found in the period 1964 through 1967 a general trend toward decreasing certainty associated with a trend of increasing criminality without any evidence that an increase in certainty would result in a decrease in crime. An operational definition of severity as the median length of sentence served indicated changes leading to the conclusion that "certainty but not severity of punishment . . . appears to be related to crime rates."

The threat of punishment is posited with a deterrent power on the assumption that the threat gets translated in the final analysis to an expectation. Essential for this translation are both certainty and severity. As Gibbs, Tittle, Chiricos and Waldo, and Teevan all point out, what is pertinent here is not the punishment that has been threatened for infraction but the punishment that has been imposed. Whether the individual is a first offender or a recidivist, the conscious or unconscious deliberations that precede an act must take into account not the imagery of a normative threat but the reality of an actual imposition. But in computing the certainty and severity of punishment, Gibbs, Tittle, and Chiricos and Waldo ignore, as far as homicide is concerned, the very important fact that the threatened punishment for homicide—which is death—has not been rendered impotent by complete nonimposition in most of the states studied.[16] This deficiency tends to affect both the certainty and severity of punishment in different states in different ways. As the measures rely so heavily on imprisonment, they have an inbuilt bias toward an inverse correlation, especially if, as the data presented by Reckless[17] show, the states that retained the death penalty and executed the largest proportion of their homicide offenders tend to have the highest homicide rates. Teevan,[18] however, assumes a decrease in severity because of the suspension of the penalty of death in Canada and, in so doing, implies an inverse correlation between the severity of punishment and frequency of the offence.

In addition to this, the manner in which certainty and severity have been computed in these studies tends to present a picture different from what certainty and severity have actually been conceived as. Whatever may be the differences in computational detail, certainty is measured in terms of the legal systems output and input with a ratio that is commonly referred to as a conviction rate. As the individual who is convicted is the individual who is certain of punishment, the use of such a ratio as a measure of certainty is both reasonable and justifiable, but it is reasonable and justifiable only if the legal process is looked on as a system in which input occurs at one point, and output occurs similarly at one and only one point. Such, however, is not the case. The legal process comprises a number of interconnected and interrelated processes where the input of the succeeding is not necessarily the output of the preceding—a fact that the "hard line" approach to crime, supported by the deterrence philosophy, appears to have recognized in its identification of the alleged failure to apprehend criminals, failure to convict criminals, and failure to incarcerate (punish) criminals as the cause of the alleged increase in criminality.[19] The certainty of punishment, consequently, is not expressible as the legal systems' final output and original input ratio. It is the result of a series of conditional probabilities involved in the movement of the individual from the initial point of entry into the final point of exit out of the legal process. Thus the certainty of punishment is the certainty that the individual would be apprehended, once apprehended would be prosecuted, once prosecuted would be convicted, and once convicted would be punished. The necessity of this stepwise computation lies first in the fact that at the output of each component process there are a number of cases that are pulled out simply because they should not have got in, and second in the fact that there is a variable time lapse in the various stages in the law enforcement machinery[20] that makes the proportion of cases in any year, solved and processed, vary with the passage of time. The use of the median length of sentence as a measure of the severity of punishment is also reasonable and justifiable. The punishment that an individual could expect to receive could well be what is inflicted on most, but it is unlikely that the possibility of receiving the maximum prescribed or the minimum inflicted did not enter into the computational picture of the individual.

The studies of Gibbs[21] and Tittle[22] have indicated that certainty and severity act, in endowing the threat of punishment with its deterrent power, not as independent and isolated forces but together intermixed and intertwined into a complex whole. Both Gibbs and Tittle have attempted to test the dependence of deterrence on both elements combined with the hypothesis that states that are below median certainty and above median severity will not have rates appreciably different from rates in states with above median certainty and below median severity—while those above median certainty and serverity will have rates lower than those with below median certainty and severity. This mode of analysis was adopted because the data utilized were not amenable to multiple correlation.[23] An alternative method that perhaps could have been used was the computation of a composite score—the expectation of punishment (the product of severity and certainty)—which could have been correlated with the homicide rate to test the hypothesis that the greater the expectation of punishment the lower would be the homicide rate. This is a hypothesis that sums the deterrence philosophy. With variation of the punishment imposed—death in some cases, imprisonment in some, and occasionally suspended sentence or probation—the computation of the composite score presents a multitude of problems. A third and perhaps best measure of the severity—certainty combination under existing conditions—would be that used by Schuessler (1952): the certainty of a particular form of punishment interpretable as the expectancy of the individual that that particular punishment would be inflicted on that person.

This study seeks to test the deterrent effect of punishment. The basic hypothesis that is being tested is that the incidence of crime will bear an inverse relationship to the punishment that violators could expect to have inflicted on them. As the anticipation of the individuals has a factual base, the expected punishment is conceived not in terms of the threatened punishment but in terms of the actual inflicted punishment that takes into consideration the probability or certainty that they will have a particular punishment inflicted on them. What is sought to be done is to compute expectancies of various punishments for a particular offence and correlate these expectancies with the incidence of that particular offence. As has been pointed out, the expectancy of a particular punishment for a particular offence is the resultant of a series of expectancies and would be computed from a series of conditional probabilities. Thus, the individual's expectancy to suffer death for homicide would be computed as the resultant of the probability that the offence is detected, the probability that the individual will be charged once the offence is detected, the probability that he or she will be convicted once charged, the probability that he or she will be sentenced to death once convicted, and the probability that the individual will be executed once sentenced to death. The expectancy of punishment that influences the commission of an act is the expectancy immediately prior to that act. If a year is conceived as a point in time (a conceptualization that is implied in the use of annual rates) the pertinent expectancy of punishment for crimes committed in any year would be the expectancy at the beginning of that year.

As the individual's expectancy of punishment is dependent on society's treatment of others who violated the law, a question that must first be answered is which violations make the significant contribution? Is it the violations during the previous year, the violations of the more recent past, the violations of a number of years, or the accumulation from the beginning of time? More pertinently, the question here is what statistics should be utilized to give a meaningful measure of the expectancy of punishment—the statistics of the previous year alone or the statistics of a number of years? The past, in its entirety, is perhaps pertinent here, but as recent events have a tendency to overshadow the distant past in the fashioning of an individual's disposition,[24] this study seeks to compute the expectancy of punishment in any year with the statistical data for the previous five years as available at the end of the fifth year. Thus, the expectancies for detection, conviction, and punishment for the commission of a crime in 1970 will be computed from the statistics revealing the fate, by the end of 1969, of crimes committed in the five years 1965, 1966, 1967, 1968, and 1969. In connection with the conception of the expectancy of punishment, it should perhaps be pointed out that Claster[25] found that delinquents and nondelinquents had the same perception of the general chances of being apprehended and the general chances of conviction after arrest. But in the case of delinquents a "magical immunity mechanism" appeared to be at work about apprehension in their own case. They perceived their personal chances of being apprehended lower than that of others. This does not vitiate the role of the concept of the expectancy of punishment in influencing criminal or deviant behaviour. It only indicates that deviants conceive of themselves as being at the lower end of a probability distribution.

The punishments whose deterrent effects are being studied here are limited to the punishments for homicide. This limitation has been predicated by the fact that the interest in deterrence expressed here is the result of an interest in a more specific interest—the deterrent effect of the penalty of death. In this connection it may be argued that the study should be of murder and not of

homicide, for death was the threatened punishment for the former and not for
the latter in Canada from where the data have been obtained. However, as
murder is the result of a post facto evaluation of an event that is essentially
homicide, the deterrent effect of the death penalty would be reflected not in
the incidence of murder but in the incidence of homicide. Evidence for the
deterrent effect of the penalty of death could be considered provided if the
expectancy of death as a punishment for homicide was negatively correlated
with the incidence of homicide. But before such a correlation is accepted as
evidence, it should perhaps be remembered that the expectancy of some other
punishment may be the potent factor. As Zimring[26] has pointed out in connection with the before-after and retentionist-abolitionist comparisons, though
the comparison is essentially one between situations where the penalty of death
existed and where it did not, in actuality the comparison is between situations
under two different threats of punishment—death and life imprisonment. Similarly here too, the expectancy of death is not the sole variable. Playing their
part are the expectancy of life imprisonment, the expectancy of other terms
of imprisonment, and the expectancy of no punishment at all.

The Dominion Bureau of Statistics has published since 1966 a wealth of
statistical information on homicides committed in Canada since 1961.[27] From
these publications the number of homicides—reported by the police as murder—
committed in the years 1961 through 1970, the cases cleared, the number of
persons charged, taken to trial, and convicted could be gleaned. Also capable
of being gleaned from the published data are the number of persons sentenced
to death (executed and commuted), sentenced to various prison terms, given
a suspended sentence, or released on probation and the number of persons
acquitted. From this data can be computed the proportion of cases cleared,
the proportion cleared by charge, the proportion of persons charged taken to
trial, the proportion of persons tried convicted or acquitted, the proportion
convicted executed, sentenced to and serving different terms of imprisonment,
given a suspended sentence, and released on probation. The information is
available in the published statistics not as a single even datum but as a series of
varying figures that reveal the procedural fate of homicide cases committed in
any year at the end of that year and the subsequent four years. From this
data the various relevant probabilities have been computed and the expectancy
of death, of life imprisonment, of other terms of imprisonment, of a suspended
sentence, of probation as punishment, and of receiving no punishment whatso-
ever for the years 1965 through 1970 have been calculated. These expectancies
are shown in Table 3-1. Also shown in Table 3-1 are the murder rates (crimes
known to the police) for those years.

The murder rate has increased from 1.5 in 1965 to 2.3 in 1970 with a fall
in 1966 to 1.3. There is a clear and distinct increase that is marked since 1968—
when the moratorium on the death penalty began. The period under consideration is too short to indicate whether this increase is due to the moratorium.

Table 3-1

Murder Rates and Expectancies of Punishment (1965-1970)

	1965	1966	1967	1968	1969	1970
Murder rate	1.5	1.3	1.6	1.8	1.9	2.3
Expectancy of:						
Death Penalty	0.2	0.2	0.1	0.0	0.0	0.0
Life Imprisonment	16.8	16.6	15.9	17.1	14.1	13.5
Other Imprisonment	20.0	18.1	19.4	21.7	22.3	24.6
Probation or Suspended						
Sentence	1.0	0.9	1.0	0.7	0.7	0.6
No Punishment	61.9	64.2	63.6	60.5	62.9	61.3
Expected Prison Term (Yrs.)	4.47	4.35	5.00	4.59	4.82	5.05

Source: Calculated from data in Dominion Bureau of Statistics: *Murder Statistics.*

The period under consideration may be the upward limb of a naturally occurring cyclical variation bearing no relation to variation in threatened or inflicted punishment. That homicide rates show such cyclical variations has been amply demonstrated.[28]

The expectancy of death as a punishment has declined during the period. The last execution in Canada was of a person who committed murder in 1962, and if the events of any year influence the expectancy picture for five years, as has been assumed in this study, this event ceases to exert any influences after 1967. In any event the enlargement of the category of noncapital murder to include almost all murders from the beginning of 1968 reduces the expectancy of death as punishment for murder from that year to almost zero. The expectancy of death correlates negatively with the murder rate ($r = -0.85$) significantly at the 5 percent level. This correlation suggests that the penalty of death does exert some deterrent effect on the incidence of murder.

With the nonexecution of murderers, the punishment for homicide becomes almost exclusively imprisonment that could take one of two forms—life or term. The expectancy of life imprisonment has shown an initial increase and a later decrease, and as must necessarily be the case the expectancy of other terms of imprisonment has shown an initial decrease and a later increase. The expectancy of life imprisonment correlates negatively with the murder rate ($r = -0.79$) but the correlation is not significant. The expectancy of other terms of imprisonment correlates positively with the murder rate ($r = +0.98$), and the correlation is significant at the 1 percent level.

The expectancy of probation or a suspended sentence has decreased and correlates with the murder rate negatively ($r = -0.80$), but the correlation is not significant. The expectancy of receiving no punishment at all has remained

more or less constant with fluctuations. This expectancy correlates negatively
($r = -0.60$) though insignificantly with the murder rate.

The data indicate that there are two expectancies that have influenced the
incidence of murder: the expectancy of death as punishment and the expectancy
of a term imprisonment as a punishment. The coefficient of multiple correlation
is 0.99. The two expectancies correlate with each other negatively ($r = -0.83$)
significant at the 5 percent level, so that the change in the incidence of murder
must be considered attributable not to the moratorium on the penalty of death
but to the substitution de facto of this penalty with term imprisonment. The
data suggest that punishment does have a deterrent effect and compels one to
conclude that there is a minimum threshold value below which punishment is
both meaningless and useless—a hypothesis that has support in the experimental
work of Bandura,[29] in which it was found that children are deterred from
indulging in behaviour perceived by them as unsuccessful or punished only to
the point that reward for such behaviour becomes too valuable to pass up.

The de facto substitution of death with term imprisonment is possible
because of an altered categorization of homicide. Murder, for which the death
penalty was threatened, carries a mandatory life imprisonment during the
moratorium. What the moratorium on the penalty of death should have done
was to increase the expectancy of life imprisonment as punishment and not the
expectancy of term imprisonment. But what has actually happened is a decrease
in the expectancy of life imprisonment and an increase in the expectancy of
term imprisonment. This could happen only if the incidence of murder, as
finally adjudicated in the courts, decreased. This decrease suggests a change that
is independent of the threatened penalty, a change in the interpretational process
occurring during court adjudication, making the offence for which death had
been threatened one that is increasingly unlikely to occur. With this change
the retention of the penalty of death would increase the severity of the threatened punishment for murder, an offence as which the act of homicide was
increasingly unlikely to be interpreted.

This analysis has proceeded from the assumption that deterrence is essentially
a psychological element dependent on the individual's perception of the reality
of things. Most studies in deterrence, Henshell and Carey[30] contend, have
ignored this important fact. Though the perception of the individual has been
considered here, the criticism of Henshel and Carey is applicable to this study as
well. The point that they make is that the objective existence of sanctions with
specified levels of severity, certainty, and swiftness is of no consequence if the
mind in question holds no cognition relative to the punitive sanction. If the
individual has not heard of, believed in, or felt applicable the punishment,
deterrence cannot exist for that individual—but not because deterrence does
not exist. Public awareness of the sanctions, they contend, as Van Den Haag
has contended earlier,[31] is a vital consideration. Variations of public awareness
of sanctions, they point out, could account for Sellin's finding that the

reintroduction of the penalty of death was followed by a decline in homicide rates in some states and a rise in others,[32] Kuykendall's finding that the association between certainty and the crime rate varied from one type of crime to another,[33] and to the finding of Chiricos and Waldo that the correlation of certainty with criminality is somewhat variable over time and highly variable among offences.[34] That public awareness of sanctions plays an important part in the deterrent question there can be no doubt. The theory of deterrence proceeds on the assumption that the public knows and this assumption is reiterated in the legal maxim "ignorance of the law is no excuse." But public awareness is pertinent to the question of deterrence only when deterrence is viewed in its abstract form: when the question sought to be answered is the theoretical "Can punishment deter?" When deterrence is viewed in its concrete form, and the question to be answered is the more practical "Does punishment deter?" public awareness of sanctions assumes a position of relative unimportance. If a deterrent effect of punishment is rendered ineffective by public ignorance of the punishment or by another factor, the punishment still fails to deter: it is impotent. For the acceptance or rejection of a theory of punishment the cause of the impotence is pertinent: for the formulation of social policy it is the fact of impotence that matters.

Notes

1. C. Beccaria (1809) *Essays on Crime and Punishment* (New York: Harper and Row).

2. See Chapter 2.

3. T. Sellin (1967) "Homicide in Retentionist and Abolitionist States," in T. Sellin: *Capital Punishment* (New York: Harper and Row) pp. 135-138.

4. J. Andennaes (1966) "The General Preventive Effects of Punishment." *Univ. Penn. Law Rev.*, 114, 949.

5. Andennaes, "General Preventive Effects," 949.

6. K. Schuessler (1952) "The Deterrent Influence of the Death Penalty." *Ann. Amer. Acad. Pol. Soc. Sci.*, 284, 54-62.

7. W. J. Chambliss (1966) "The Deterrent Influence of Punishment." *Crime Delinq.*, 12, 70-75.

8. J. Andennaes (1952) "General Prevention. Illusion or Reality." *Jour. Crim. Law Criminol.*, 43, 176-178; J. Toby (1964) "Is Punishment Necessary." *Jour. Crim. Law Criminol.*, 55, 332-337.

9. G. Tarde (1912) *Penal Philosophy* (Boston: Little, Brown).

10. J. P. Gibbs (1968) "Crime Punishment and Deterrence." *Southwestern Soc. Sci. Quart.*, 48, 515-530.

11. C. R. Tittle (1969) "Crime Rates and Legal Sanctions." *Soc. Prob.,* 16, 409-423.

12. Gibbs "Crime Punishment and Deterrence," 515-530.

13. Tittle "Crime Rates," 409-423.

14. T. G. Chiricos and G. P. Waldo (1970) "Punishment and Crime. An Examination of Some Empirical Evidence." *Soc. Prob.,* 18, 200-217.

15. J. J. Teevan (1972) "Deterrent Effects of Punishment: The Canadian Case." *Canad. Jour. Criminol. Correct.,* 14, 68-82.

16. Chiricos and Waldo, "Punishment and Crime," 200-217.

17. W. C. Reckless (1969) "The Use of the Death Penalty." *Crime Delinq.,* 15, 43-56.

18. Teevan, "Deterrent Effects of Punishment," 68-82.

19. F. E. Inbau and F. G. Carrington (1971) "The Case of the So-Called Hard Line Approach to Crime." *Ann. Amer. Acad. Pol. Soc. Sci.,* 397, 19-27.

20. C. H. S. Jayewardene and H. Ranasinghe (1961) *Criminal Homicide in the Southern Province* (Colombo: Colombo Apothecaries Co., Ltd.).

21. Gibbs, "Crime Punishment and Deterrence," 515-530.

22. Tittle, "Crime Rates," 409-423.

23. Gibbs, "Crime Punishment and Deterrence," 515-530.

24. C. H. S. Jayewardene (1971) *Value Change of Emergent Youth in Ceylon.* Paper. Conference on Population Growth, the Human Condition and Politics in South East Asia. New York. Columbia University, November.

25. D. Claster (1967) "Comparison of Risk Perception between Delinquents and Non-Delinquents." *Jour. Crim. Law Criminol.,* 58, 80.

26. F. Zimring (1971) *Perspectives on Deterrence* (Washington, D.C.: Government Printing Office).

27. Dominion Bureau of Statistics (1967) *Murder Statistics 1961-1965* (Ottawa: Queen's Printer). Dominion Bureau of Statistics (1967) *Murder Statistics 1966* (Ottawa: Queen's Printer). Dominion Bureau of Statistics (1968) *Murder Statistics 1967* (Ottawa: Queen's Printer). Dominion Bureau of Statistics (1969) *Murder Statistics 1968* (Ottawa: Queen's Printer). Dominion Bureau of Statistics (1970) *Murder Statistics 1969* (Ottawa: Queen's Printer). Dominion Bureau of Statistics (1971) *Murder Statistics 1970* (Ottawa: Queen's Printer).

28. A. F. Henry and J. F. Short (1954) *Suicide and Homicide* (Glencoe, Ill.: The Free Press). D. S. Thomas (1927) *Social Aspects of the Business Cycle* (New York: A. A. Knopf). C. H. S. Jayewardene (1960) "Criminal Homicide: A Study in Culture Conflict," (Unpublished Ph.D. Thesis. University of Pennsylvania).

29. A. Bandura (1965) "Influence of Model's Reinforcement Contingencies on the Acquisition of Imitative Responses." *Jour. Personality Soc. Psychol.,* 1, 589-595.

30. R. L. Henshel and S. H. Carey (1972) *Deviance, Deterrence and Knowledge of Sanctions.* Paper. Eastern Sociological Society Meetings. Boston, April.

31. E. Van Den Haag (1969) "On Deterrence and the Death Penalty." *Jour. Crim. Law Criminol.,* 60, 141-147.

32. T. Sellin, "Homicide in Retentionist and Abolitionist States," 135-138.

33. H. K. Kuykendall (1969) "The Deterrent Efficacy of Punishment." (Unpublished Master's Thesis. University of Texas).

34. Chiricos and Waldo, "Punishment and Crime," 200-217.

4

Murder 1961-1970—Before and
After the Moratorium

In the study of murder over a period of time, criminologists are frequently committed to the use of officially published data. Criminal statistics for Canada—relating to murder—have been collected since Confederation,[1] but the Joint Committee of the Senate and the House of Commons on Capital Punishment, Corporal Punishment and Lotteries[2] reported that the figures were not only incomplete but also were gathered by various agencies that were not related to one another—a procedure that vitiated their meaningful use. In 1961, the Dominion Bureau of Statistics, in consultation with all the Provinces and the Department of Justice, started a detailed study of homicide in Canada.[3] The need for accurate information led to improved data collection techniques that also ensured more complete coverage. While the Dominion Bureau of Statistics' study on homicide continues, the public has been offered in an annual published document entitled *Murder Statistics*—a picture of the situation in Canada. It is the data presented in these documents that are analyzed here. Published statistics do have many shortcomings, but yet, those described as "crimes known to the police," which the murder statistics published by the Dominion Bureau of Statistics essentially are, present the best picture of the situation; and, as murder is a crime that has a high reportability, the picture obtained is not only the best possible but also very near the actual situation.[4] Yet, in their 1970 publication, the Dominion Bureau of Statistics issues a word of caution to users of their data. It is contended that the publication covers murder as reported by the police and that the police lay a charge of murder only on the instructions of the Crown Prosecutor. As the Criminal Code definition of murder has changed three times since 1961, the user of the data is cautioned that behavioural research based on them may be affected.[5]

The Criminal Code defines murder as culpable homicide

(a) Where the person who causes the death of a human being
     (i)   means to cause his death, or
     (ii) means to cause him bodily harm that he knows is likely to cause death and is reckless whether death ensues or not;
(b) where a person meaning to cause death . . . or meaning to cause bodily harm that he knows is likely to cause death, and being reckless whether it ensues or not, by accident or mistake causes death of another human being, not withstanding that he does not mean to cause death or bodily harm to that human being; or
(c) where a person, for an unlawful object does anything that he knows or

33

ought to know is likely to cause death . . . not withstanding that he desires
to effect his object without causing death or bodily harm to any human
being" (Section 201).

Culpable homicide is also defined as murder where the death is caused

while committing or attempting to commit treason or an offence mentioned in
Section 52, piracy, escape or rescue from lawful custody, resisting lawful arrest,
rape, indecent assault, forcible abduction, robbery, burglary or arson, whether
or not the person means to cause death to any human being and whether or not
death is likely to be caused to any human being if
(a)   he means to cause bodily harm for the purpose of
        (i)   facilitating the commission of the offence;
        (ii)   facilitating the flight after committing or attempting to commit
                the offence, and the death ensues from the bodily harm;
(b)   he administers a stupefying or overpowering thing for a purpose mentioned
        in (a) and death ensues therefrom; or
(c)   he wilfully stops, by any means, the breath of a human being for the pur-
        pose mentioned in (a) and death ensues therefrom; or
(d)   he uses a weapon or has it on his person
        (i)   during or at the time he commits or attempts to commit the offence;
                or
        (ii)   during or at the time of his flight after committing or attempting to
                commit the offence, and death ensues as a consequence" (Section
                202).

Prior to 1961 all murder carried the mandatory death penalty. After 1961
murder was categorizable into capital murder (premeditated murder, the murder
of a police officer, prison officer, etc., and murder during the commission of
another criminal act) carrying the mandatory death penalty and noncapital
murder carrying the mandatory sentence of life imprisonment. In December
1967 further amendments were made (for a five-year trial period) redefining
capital and noncapital murder. As it stands today, murder is defined as capital
murder where

"a person by his own act caused or assisted in causing the death of
(a)   a police officer, police constable, constable sheriff, deputy sheriff, sheriff's
        officer or other person employed for the preservation and maintenance
        of the public peace, acting in the course of his duties;
(b)   a warden, deputy warden, instructor, keeper, gaoler, guard or other officer
        or permanent employee of a prison, acting in the course of his duties; or
        counselled or procured another person to any act causing or assisting in
        causing death" (Section 202 A)

Homicide—the killing of a human being by another human being—is usually
looked on by the general public as murder. But all homicide is not legally defined
as murder; neither is all culpable homicide. Some culpable homicide may

constitute the offence of manslaughter (Section 207) and some the offence of infanticide (Section 206). Variations in murder statistics can stem not from variations in the categorization of murder into capital and noncapital, but from variations in the categorization of homicide as murder, be it capital or noncapital, manslaughter, or infanticide—a variation that has no change in legal definition as base. It is perhaps pertinent to point out here that there is a terminological confusion in the reporting of data that gets confounded by ignoring it in the interpretation. What is published by the Dominion Bureau of Statistics as murder statistics are not statistics of murder nor statistics of criminal homicide— all cases where the death of an individual presumably caused by another could result in the conviction of that second individual of murder, manslaughter, or even a lesser crime—but statistics of homicide designated by the police as murder. These cases are investigated by the police as murder and frequently, the offence with which such an individual is charged is murder. Herein lies the justification for labelling such statistics murder statistics.

Homicide is the only crime whose incidence is reported by two independent and unrelated agencies. There are, in every country, two sets of statistics referring to this problem—the police or criminal statistics and the death or vital statistics. Comparison of the two sets of statistics[6] has revealed dissimilarities. Vold, who compared the two sets in the United States, attributed the dissimilarity to differences in areal coverage. When the areal coverage became similar, he contended, the two sets of statistics would be similar.[7] Jayewardene compared the two sets in Ceylon, Finland, and England and Wales, where differences in areal coverage did not exist, but where differences in the statistics nevertheless existed. His study led to the identification of an additional component— the definition of the counting unit. Usually the vital statistics should record more homicides than the police statistics, because the former include in their figures accidental manslaughters and justifiable homicides. Frequently, however, the police figures are higher. This happens because the police counting is done prior to the final decision as to the nature of the event, forcing the inclusion of cases that are finally not adjudicated homicide. When the police count is made after the adjudication process decides the nature of the event, as has been the case in Finland, there is a marked similarity in the two sets of statistics.[8]

The *Murder Statistics* of the Dominion Bureau of Statistics give the number and rates of murder as reported to them by the police and of homicidal deaths as officially recorded on provincial death certificates reported to them from 1954 onwards. The murder figures before 1961 do not include those committed in Quebec: since 1961 they refer to all murders committed in the country. The homicide figures, presented for comparison, have been made comparable to the murder figures by the exclusion of accidental manslaughters and homicides resulting from the intervention of police and legal executions.[9] As the murder figures exclude infanticides, which are included in the homicide figures, the two sets of statistics refer to different phenomena—most criminal homicide in the one case and all culpable homicide in the other. The importance of recognizing this difference lies in the claim that: "the increase in the number of murders since 1960, indicated by figures, could be explained by better reporting and coverage of the crime reporting program, since rates for murder and homicidal deaths were becoming identical."[10]

The two sets of figures for Canada[11] are given in Table 4-1. The figures indicate a tendency for the two sets to converge. As the murder figures prior to 1961 were exclusive of the events in Quebec, the dissimilarity in the two sets of figures prior to 1961 could be explained in terms of areal coverage. With the inclusion of the Quebec figures since 1961 the dissimilarity is explainable only in definitional terms. If the vital statistics figures represent an accurate count of culpable homicides in the country, the murder figures suggest an increasing tendency to label all culpable homicides as murder. This tendency lends itself to the hypothesis that associated with legal changes in the penalty of death were

Table 4-1
Murder and Homicide Rates (1954-1970)[a]

Year	Murder[b]	Homicide[c]	Proportion of homicide reported as murder[d]
1954	1.0	1.2	83.3
1955	0.9	1.2	75.0
1956	1.0	1.3	76.9
1957	0.9	1.2	75.0
1958	1.1	1.4	78.6
1959	1.0	1.2	83.3
1960	1.3	1.6	81.3
1961	1.2	1.4	85.7
1962	1.4	1.6	87.5
1963	1.4	1.5	93.3
1964	1.4	1.5	93.3
1965	1.5	1.6	93.8
1966	1.3	1.5	86.7
1967	1.6	1.8	88.9
1968	1.8	1.8	100.0
1969	1.9	2.1	90.5
1970	2.3	na	

Source: The annual publication of the Dominion Bureau of Statistics: *Murder Statistics*, Table 1.

[a]Rates are per 100,000 population 7 years and over.

[b]Murder rates — reported by the police as murder.

[c]Homicide rates — reported on provincial death certificates as homicide but excludes those recorded as accidental and justifiable homicides.

[d]1954-1960 murder rates exclude events in Quebec but homicide rates include them.

procedural changes in the Prosecutor's office whereby "a charge of non-capital murder would have been lesser at a time when the alternative was capital murder."[12] The observed convergence of these two sets of statistics could be theoretically explained in terms of better reporting and coverage, but then the two figures could only become similar if infanticides ceased to occur factually or definitionally.

Both the murder and homicide rates as reported by the Dominion Bureau of Statistics show an increase during the period 1954 through 1970. In 1954 the murder rate was 1.0 and the homicide rate 1.2. The figures remained more or less constant till 1960, when an increase to 1.3 and 1.6 respectively was recorded. Since 1960, the murder rate has shown an increase—at first slight—fluctuating around 1.4, but more marked since 1967 when the murder rate increased to 1.6, and in subsequent years to 1.8, 1.9, and 2.3. The homicide rate too has increased since 1960. During the period 1961 through 1967, it fluctuated between 1.4 and 1.6, in 1968 and 1969 it was 1.8, and in 1970 it was 2.1. But what do these increasing figures indicate?

The murder and homicide rates refer to deaths and in doing so give the number of victims per 100,000 population. The common assumption that homicide is a phenomenon where the number of events, offenders, and victims are collectively the same has endowed murder and homicide rates with a connotation that leads to their interpretation as representing the probability that an individual would become a homicide offender or victim. Such an interpretation, however, is erroneous in as much as some segments of the population, in age and sex terms, are more likely to become homicide offenders or victims than others. Thus, a child under seven years of age because of legal incapacity to possess mens rea is incapable of committing criminal homicide, and again women and the aged, though legally able, are either physically unable or socially unlikely to commit homicide.[13]

The offender and victim rates for the different age-sex groups in Canada 1961-1970 (Tables 4-2 and 4-3) show that the likelihood of becoming an offender or victim of murder in Canada is not the same for all age groups. For both males and females the highest offender rates are for the age group "20-29 years old." The rates for the age groups "30-39 years old" and "40-49 years old" are lower but still much higher than the rates for the age groups "under 20 years old" and "over 50 years old." The female rates are much lower than the male rates. The rates have shown an increase over time in the younger age groups. In the males the increase is most marked in the "under 20 years old" age group and in the females in the "30-39 years old" one. As in the case of the offenders, the victim rates are lower for females than for males, but the difference here is much less pronounced. The highest rate for males was, at the beginning of the period under study, in the "30-39 years old" age group followed by the "over 50 years old" group but the increases over time have altered the picture somewhat to give pride of place to the "20-29 years old"

Table 4-2
Murder Offender Rates for Different Age-Sex Groups (1961-1970)

Year	Under 19 Yrs.		20-29 Years		30-39 Years		40-49 Years		Over 50 Yrs.	
	Male	Female	Male	Female	Male	Female	Male	Female	Male	Female
1961	0.62	0.05	3.41	0.75	2.98	0.47	2.42	0.28	1.47	0.00
1962	0.63	0.05	3.57	0.75	4.23	0.39	1.74	0.09	1.22	0.27
1963	0.51	0.00	5.91	0.65	3.93	0.47	2.88	0.27	1.03	0.00
1964	0.65	0.02	5.22	0.40	3.78	0.56	1.68	0.43	0.90	0.05
1965	1.20	0.12	4.67	0.46	3.78	0.72	2.78	0.17	1.36	0.00
1966	1.65	0.07	5.72	1.25	3.44	0.48	1.71	0.33	0.97	0.00
1967	1.15	0.00	5.53	0.34	4.19	1.11	1.34	0.24	1.10	0.09
1968	1.67	0.11	6.82	0.52	4.65	1.03	2.14	0.32	1.28	0.46
1969	1.67	0.07	6.76	1.00	4.25	1.26	2.67	0.40	1.16	0.13
1970	na	na	na	na	na	na	na	na	na	na

Source: Calculated from data in the annual publications of the Dominion Bureau of Statistics: *Murder Statistics*, Table 11, and *Vital Statistics*, Table S4.

Notes: Rates are per million population in each group. Population data for 1970 are not available for the calculation of the rates for that year.

Table 4-3
Murder Victim Rates for Different Age-Sex Groups (1961-1970)

Year	Under 20 Yrs.		20-29 Years		30-39 Years		40-49 Years		Over 50 Yrs.	
	Male	Female	Male	Female	Male	Female	Male	Female	Male	Female
1961	0.28	0.29	1.33	1.25	2.11	1.19	1.76	1.51	2.14	0.95
1962	0.50	0.49	1.82	1.66	2.42	1.73	1.64	1.38	1.99	0.76
1963	0.48	0.53	2.38	1.72	1.88	1.19	1.53	1.35	1.79	1.06
1964	0.35	0.45	2.08	1.85	2.04	1.68	2.12	1.23	1.80	0.88
1965	0.58	0.66	1.94	1.87	2.20	1.05	1.91	1.89	2.18	0.75
1966	0.62	0.50	1.85	1.69	2.26	0.96	1.28	1.35	1.40	1.07
1967	0.66	0.91	2.24	1.74	2.48	1.59	2.17	1.82	1.80	0.99
1968	0.68	0.69	2.38	2.44	2.86	1.43	2.71	1.46	2.21	1.38
1969	0.91	0.64	3.62	1.94	3.16	1.89	3.31	1.12	2.17	0.94
1970	na	na	na	na	na	na	na	na	na	na

Source: Calculated from data in the annual publications of the Dominion Bureau of Statistics: *Murder Statistics*, Table 14, and *Vital Statistics*, Table S4.

Notes: Rates are per million population in age group. Population data for 1970 are not available for the calculation of the rates for that year.

age group and the "40-49 years old" group. Among the females the highest rates were in the "20-29 years old" and "40-49 years old" age groups. This was at the beginning of the period under study. At the end of the period the age groups "20-29 years old" and "30-39 years old" had the highest rates.

Murder, and all homicide as well, has been regarded as a highly personalized type of crime, where the offender and the victim have some previous association frequently of a primary nature.[14] But all murders and homicides do not fall into this category. Strangers do sometimes get killed. They get killed when a mentally unbalanced individual goes on a murder rampage but more frequently during the commission of another offence by the offender. Consequently there appears to be at least two distinct types of murder or homicide. There is first the personalized type—where there is a prior close relationship between the offender and the victim and where the event itself is fired with a high love-hate emotional content. There is then the impersonalized type—where the offender and victim were unacquainted and the event void of the emotional content that makes it personalized. Homicide studies seem to indicate that the personalized type predominates. A survey of the literature shows that in half to three-fourths of the cases there has been some prior association between the offender and the victim.[15] This proportion, however, varies from time to time and from place to place. Wolfgang found in his study of homicides committed in Philadelphia the "stranger" relationship in 13 percent of his 588 cases,[16] and in a national survey of cities in the United States in which 20.9 percent of the victim-offender relationships were described as unknown, 15.6 percent of the homicides involved strangers.[17]

The Dominion Bureau of Statistics recognizes the existence of three types of murder. On the basis of the relationship between the offender and the victim, they categorize murder as "domestic" when the victim was a member of the immediate or extended family of the offender and "nondomestic" when no such victim-offender relationship existed. The latter is further divided into two groups. Into one, labelled "criminal act," fall murders committed during the commission of another crime and into the other, labelled "nondomestic other," murders where the accused was insane, where the killing was that of a non-family member following an argument with or without drink, and where it was professionally carried out as a deliberate act in itself unassociated with the commission of any other crime. This categorization differs from the personalized and impersonalized division of murders and homicides, although the domestic/nondomestic division is akin to it. However, the "nondomestic" group contains some cases that would fall into the personalized category that is the equivalent of the domestic group.

The Dominion Bureau of Statistics has considered the categorization sufficiently significant to make it the subject of two special studies. In the first[18] the focus of attention was on the relationship between the gravity of the offence as revealed in the final adjudication and the victim-offender relationship. In this

Table 4-4
Method of Killing According to Type of Murder (1961-1970)

| | Type of Murder | | |
Method of Killing	Domestic[a]	Criminal[b]	Nondomestic Other[c]
Shooting	542	135	501
Beating	233	123	243
Stabbing	176	63	213
Strangulation	61	43	74
Suffocation	24	11	14
Explosive	4	3	3
Drowning	21	2	4
Arson	12	46	8
Other	29	9	25
Unknown	7	10	26
Total	1109	445	1111

Source: The annual publication of the Dominion Bureau of Statistics: *Murder Statistics*, Table 15.

Note: X^2 = 210.4 (significant at 1 percent level).

[a]Domestic murders are murders in which the victim is a member of the immediate or extended family of the offender.

[b]Criminal Act murders are those committed during the commission of another crime.

[c]Nondomestic other" category contains all other murders.

study it was found that the "criminal act" category, while constituting the smallest group, carried the highest chance of conviction—and conviction of the more serious offence. The second study[19] focused its attention on the "criminal act" category of murder describing in detail its frequency, the other crimes that are associated with the murder, and the age and sex distribution of the offenders and the victims. A graphical comparison of the three types of murder during the period 1961-1970 indicates an increase in the number falling into each category over the total period with a sharp increase in the "criminal act" category since the moratorium on the penalty of death. The increase in the "nondomestic other" category was greater than that in the "domestic category."

Further evidence for the difference in these types of murder could perhaps be adduced by analysis of the age-sex distribution of victims and offenders, the method used in killing, and the season of the year in which the homicide is committed, statistical data for which are given in the annual publication *Murder*

Table 4-5
Season of Year in which Murder Is Committed (1961-1970)

| | Type of Murder | | |
Season	Domestic[a]	Criminal Act[b]	Nondomestic Other[c]
Spring	217	96	227
Summer	251	96	287
Autumn	246	107	271
Winter	237	86	233
Unknown	0	1	9
Total	951	386	1027

Source: The annual publication of the Dominion Bureau of Statistics: *Murder Statistics,* Table 16.

Note: X^2 = 13.01 (not significant).

[a]Domestic murders are homicides in which the victim is a member of the immediate or extended family of the offender.

[b]Criminal Act murders are those committed during the commission of another crime.

[c]Nondomestic other category contains all other murders.

Statistics. The three commonest methods used for killing, whatever the type of murder may be, are shooting, beating, and stabbing (Table 4-4). These three methods account for 85.9 percent of the "domestic" homicides, 72.99 percent of the "criminal act" type, and 86.13 percent of the "nondomestic other" type. The distribution of the cases into the other methods of killing is sufficiently different to be statistically significant (X^2 = 210.4). The season during which the murders are committed (Table 4-5) does not help to differentiate the type of murder. Approximately an equal proportion of the murders are committed in each season. Statistical tests here indicate no significant difference (X^2 = 13.0). The age and sex distribution of offenders (Table 4-6) and victims (Table 4-7) show marked differences for the different types of murders. The offenders in both the "nondomestic" murder groups are almost entirely male. They constitute 96.4 percent of the offenders in the "criminal act" category and 94.9 percent in the "nondomestic other" one. In the "domestic" category males constitute 78.6 percent of the offenders. A larger proportion of offenders fall into the younger age groups in the "nondomestic" than in the "domestic" homicides. The age distribution is significantly different in the case of males (X^2 = 194.1), but the difference is not significant in the case of females. Among the victims too the male preponderance in the "nondomestic" murders is evident. Males constitute 69.7 percent of the victims in the "criminal act" category and

Table 4-6
Age and Sex Distribution of Offenders According to Type of Murder
(1961-1970)

	Type of Murder		
	---	---	---
Age Group	Domestic[a]	Criminal Act[b]	Nondomestic Other[c]
Under 20 Years			
Male	92	110	144
Female	18	2	8
Total	110	112	152
20-29 Years			
Male	175	191	389
Female	68	7	22
Total	243	198	411
30-39 Years			
Male	212	85	217
Female	69	4	17
Total	281	89	234
40-49 Years			
Male	139	25	95
Female	34	1	2
Total	173	26	97
Over 50 Years			
Male	124	9	93
Female	12	2	0
Total	136	11	93
Unknown			
Male	13	7	4
Female	4	0	2
Total	17	7	6
Total			
Male	775	427	942
Female	205	17	51
Total	960	442·	993

Source: Annual publications of the Dominion Bureau of Statistics: *Murder Statistics*, Table 11.

Notes: Age (Male) $X^2 = 194.14$ (significant at 1 percent level).
Age (Female) $X^2 = 14.85$ (not significant)
Age (Total) $X^2 = 190.6$ (significant at 1 percent level).

[a]Domestic murders are murders in which the victim is a member of the immediate or extended family of the offender.

[b]Criminal Act murders are those committed during the commission of another crime.

[c]Nondomestic other category contains all other murders.

Table 4-7
Age and Sex Distribution of Victims According to Type of Murder (1961-1970)

| Age Group | Type of Murder | | |
	Domestic[a]	Criminal Act[b]	Nondomestic Other[c]
Under 20 Years			
Male	147	18	92
Female	132	32	84
Total	279	50	176
20-29 Years			
Male	59	40	213
Female	154	24	83
Total	213	64	296
30-39 Years			
Male	79	44	204
Female	134	16	35
Total	213	60	239
40-49 Years			
Male	78	49	129
Female	130	14	30
Total	208	63	159
Over 50 Years			
Male	85	159	168
Female	111	48	69
Total	196	207	237
Unknown			
Male	0	0	4
Female	0	1	0
Total	0	1	4
Total			
Male	448	310	810
Female	661	135	301
Total	1109	445	1111

Source: Annual publication of the Dominion Bureau of Statistics: *Murder Statistics,* Table 14.

Notes: Age (Male) $X^2 = 254.56$ (significant at 1 percent level).
Age (Female) $X^2 = 63.46$ (significant at 1 percent level).
Age (Total) $X^2 = 207.41$ (significant at 1 percent level).

[a]Domestic murders are murders in which the victim is a member of the immediate or extended family of the offender.

[b]Criminal Act murders are those committed during the commission of another crime.

[c]Nondomestic other category contains all other murders.

Table 4-8
Types of Murders (1961-1970)

Year	Domestic[a]	Criminal Act[b]	Nondomestic[c]	Total[d]
		Type of Murder		
1961	50.29	16.18	33.53	173
1962	43.88	22.96	33.16	196
1963	42.49	19.17	38.34	193
1964	38.19	20.10	41.71	199
1965	38.60	14.88	46.52	215
1966	44.61	16.18	39.21	204
1967	39.50	9.67	30.83	238
1968	40.48	12.80	46.72	289
1969	38.10	13.65	38.25	315
1970	32.77	19.08	48.15	351
r (Time)	-0.77	-0.46	0.87	

Source: Annual publication of the Dominion Bureau of Statistics: *Murder Statistics,*
Table 14.

Note: X^2 = 49.80 (significant at 5 percent level).

[a]Domestic murders are murders in which the victim is a member of the immediate or
extended family of the offender.

[b]Criminal Act murders are those committed during the commission of another crime.

[c]The nondomestic category contains all other murders.

[d]Figures are percentages of the total falling into each category in that year. The totals are
incidents and not offenders or victims.

73.2 percent in the "nondomestic other" category. In the "domestic" category
they constitute 40.4 percent of the victims. The age distribution shows a significant difference in the case of males (X^2 = 254.6) as well as in the case of
females (X^2 = 63.5).

The proportions of the murders that fall into the different categories
(Table 4-8) indicate that there is a change in the nature of murder in Canada.
In 1961 the "domestic" or personalized type of murders constituted 50.29
percent of all homicides. Since this date there has been a decrease in the
proportion falling into this category till in 1970 the proportion was 32.77 percent. The proportions correlate significantly with time (r = —.77) indicating a
definite decreasing trend. The "nondomestic other" category has shown an
increase. In 1961 the proportion falling into this category was 33.53 percent.
The figure in 1970 was 48.15 percent. The proportions too correlate signifi-

cantly with time (r = .87) indicating a definite increasing trend. Variations have occurred in the proportion falling into the "criminal act" variety, but these variations take the form of erratic fluctuations rather than a discernible trend (r = 0.46). Taken together the variation in the proportions falling into the different categories are statistically significant (X^2 = 49.8) providing evidence for the changing nature of homicide in Canada.

Notes

1. Dominion Bureau of Statistics (1967) *Murder Statistics 1961-1965* (Ottawa: Queen's Printer).

2. Joint Committee of the Senate and House of Commons on Capital Punishment, Corporal Punishment and Lotteries (1956) *Report* (Ottawa: Queen's Printer).

3. Dominion Bureau of Statistics, *Murder Statistics 1961-1965.*

4. T. Sellin (1937) *Research Memorandum on Crime in the Depression* (New York: Social Science Research Council).

5. Dominion Bureau of Statistics (1970) *Murder Statistics 1969* (Ottawa: Queen's Printer).

6. C. H. S. Jayewardene (1960) "Criminal Homicide. A Study in Culture Conflict." (Unpublished Ph.D. Thesis. University of Pennsylvania); G. B. Vold (1952) "Extent and Trend of Capital Crimes in the United States." *Annals Amer. Acad. Pol. Soc. Sci.,* 284, 1-7.

7. Vold, "Extent of Capital Crimes," 1-7.

8. Jayewardene, "Criminal Homicide."

9. Dominion Bureau of Statistics, *Murder Statistics 1961-1965*; Dominion Bureau of Statistics (1967) *Murder Statistics 1966* (Ottawa: Queen's Printer); Dominion Bureau of Statistics (1968) *Murder Statistics 1967* (Ottawa: Queen's Printer); Dominion Bureau of Statistics (1969) *Murder Statistics 1968* (Ottawa: Queen's Printer); Dominion Bureau of Statistics, *Murder Statistics 1969*; Dominion Bureau of Statistics (1971) *Murder Statistics 1970* (Ottawa: Queen's Printer).

10. Dominion Bureau of Statistics, *Murder Statistics 1969.*

11. In this connection it is interesting to note that the homicide figures (deaths officially recorded so on provincial death certificates) as presented in the Dominion Bureau of Statistics' publication *Murder Statistics* is different from those published in their publication *Vital Statistics.*

12. L. McDonald (1969) "Crime and Punishment in Canada. A Statistical Test of the Conventional Wisdom." *Canad. Rev. Sociol. Anthropol.,* 6, 212-236; _____(1971) "Is the Crime Rate Increasing?" in C. L. Boydell, G. F. Grindstaff, and P. C. Whitehead, *Critical Issues in Canadian Society* (Toronto: Holt Rinehart and Winston of Canada Ltd.) 467-478.

13. Jayewardene, "Criminal Homicide;" M. E. Wolfgang (1958) *Patterns in Criminal Homicide* (Philadelphia: University of Pennsylvania Press).

14. W. Goode (1969) "Violence among Intimates," in D. J. Mulvihill, M. M. Tumin, and L. A. Curtis, *Crimes of Violence* (Washington, D.C.: Government Printing Office) 941-977.

15. A. Normandeau (1968) "Trends and Patterns of Crimes of Robbery" (Unpublished Ph.D. Thesis. University of Pennsylvania).

16. Wolfgang, *Patterns in Criminal Homicide.*

17. President's Commission on Crime in the District of Columbia (1967) *Report* (Washington, D.C.: Government Printing Office); D. J. Mulvihill, M. M. Tumin, and L. A. Curtis (1969) *Crimes of Violence* (Washington, D.C.: Government Printing Office) "The Offender and His Victim," pp. 207-258.

18. Dominion Bureau of Statistics, *Murder Statistics 1967.*

19. Dominion Bureau of Statistics, *Murder Statistics 1970.*

5

Changes in the Pattern of Murder

The analysis of murder statistics during the period 1961-1970 indicates that
there has been an increase in the incidence of murder in Canada over the whole
period. This increase was slow at first, gaining momentum since 1967. Associated with this increase has been a change in the age and sex distribution of both
offenders and victims. In addition to this there appears to be a change in the
nature of murder. If the victim-offender relationship is utilized to categorize
murder as domestic, nondomestic other, and nondomestic: committed in the
commission of another crime, a smaller increase is noted in the domestic category than in the other two categories. The proportion of cases falling into the
domestic category shows a definite decreasing trend, while the proportion falling
into the nondomestic other category shows a definite increasing trend. The proportion falling into the category nondomestic in the commission of another
crime too shows an increase, but statistical analysis does not justify the identification of the increase as a trend.[1] The statistical data on which these conclusions were based are those published by the Dominion Bureau of Statistics. The
conclusions, it will be realized, are valid only to the extent that the published
statistics portray the factual situation. The thoroughness with which the Bureau
appears to have performed its task and the richness of the data it presents does
not permit any other conclusion than that the data present a picture as factual
as possible. Even if this were not so, the analysis and conclusions are relevant,
for then the data become, in their variation from fact, the picture officially
painted for public consumption.

The data indicate that there is an increase in criminal homicide in Canada.
This increase began before the moratorium on the penalty of death, but, since
the moratorium, the increase has been more marked. While this finding suggests
a deterrent effect of the penalty of death, there are other changes that have
occurred that need to be considered. The most important of these changes is
the nature of the homicide act. The age and sex distribution of offenders and
victims indicates that there is a change in the type of people who are killing and
who are being killed.

The age and sex variations in the likelihood of being a homicide offender or
victim have led to the contention that a more meaningful measure of homicidal
behaviour in society is the risk that an individual runs of becoming a homicide
offender or victim.[2] These risks are computed by aging a cohort using the age-
and sex-specific rates for a given year. The figures thus obtained give the
probability that individuals would become offenders or victims of homicide if

50 THE PENALTY OF DEATH

they lived their whole lives under the conditions reflected in the age- and sex-
specific rates for that year. These figures eliminate the influence of the structure
of a population on homicide rates and say precisely what the conventional rates
purport to say, and, in doing so, measure better the changing picture.

The risk of becoming a homicide offender (homicide potential) or a homicide victim (homicide risk) of males, females, and individuals irrespective of sex,
in Canada 1961-1970, are shown in Table 5-1. Both the homicide potential
and homicide risk of females are lower than that of males. The homicide potential of females is much lower than their homicide risk indicating, as other
studies have shown,[3] that a female is more likely to be killed than to kill. The
changes over time in Canada, however, indicate that their likelihood to kill has
increased much more than their likelihood to be killed. Among males, the homicide potential is greater than the homicide risk. They are more likely to kill than
to be killed. During the period under study both the homicide potential and the
homicide risk of males have increased, but the homicide risk—the likelihood of

Table 5-1
Homicide Potential and Homicide Risk (1961-1970)

| Year | Homicide Potential[a] | | | Homicide Risk[b] | | |
	Male	Female	Total	Male	Female	Total
1961	12.99[c]	1.60	7.35	10.06[c]	6.42	8.25
1962	13.14	1.60	7.42	10.81	7.27	9.05
1963	15.80	1.39	8.66	10.33	7.27	9.05
1964	13.78	1.53	7.70	10.54	7.42	8.99
1965	16.35	1.59	9.02	11.57	7.63	9.61
1966	16.11	2.20	9.26	9.43	7.14	8.33
1967	15.56	1.87	8.74	11.81	8.95	10.38
1968	17.51	3.01	10.28	13.73	9.47	11.60
1969	19.34	3.06	11.22	16.25	8.13	12.20
1970	na	na	na	na	na	na

Source: Calculated from the data presented in Tables 4-1 and 4-2.

[a]Homicide Potential: the probability that an individual would become a homicide offender
in lifetime if he or she lived life under the conditions reflected in the age-specific rates of
that year.

[b]Homicide Risk: the probability that an individual would become a homicide victim in
lifetime if he or she lived life under the conditions reflected in the age-specific rates of that
year.

[c]Figures are a chance in a million.

being killed—has shown a greater increase than the homicide potential—the likelihood of killing.

Female participation in crimes of violence, Verkko[4] found, tended to remain more or less constant throughout long periods of time. On the basis of this observation he formulated two laws relating the male-female ratio to the incidence of violence in a country. In the first law, which he called the "static law," he contends that "in countries of high frequency of crimes against life, the participation of women in these crimes is small and vice versa, in countries of low frequency of crimes against life, the participation of women in these crimes is perceptibly larger than in countries of high frequency of crimes against life . . . " What this law implies is that criminality, as far as crimes against life are concerned, could be measured by the male-female ratio. A high ratio indicates high criminality and a low ratio a low criminality. Also implicit in this law is the suggestion that each society, because of its own peculiar social structure, generates a minimum number of homicides, which is reflected in the female participation in crimes against life. These crimes could be looked on as necessary or nonpreventable. Day-to-day variations in social conditions produce changes responsible for additions to this minimum quantity—the preventable homicides—for whose contribution males are mainly responsible.

The second law, which he calls the "dynamic law," elaborates on this latter suggestion. It states that "if the frequency of crimes against life in a country tends to increase, the increase primarily affects male criminals and, vice versa, if the frequency of crimes against life in a certain country is on the decline, the decline primarily affects the number of male criminals." No work has been done to empirically test these laws, but some support appears to exist for Verkko's hypotheses in the statistical evidence from the United States, and from England and Wales, Africa, and Ceylon.[5]

The male-female ratios of homicide offenders, homicide victims, and homicide participants (offenders and victims combined) in Canada are shown in Table 5-2. The ratio for victims and participants has remained more or less constant during the period under consideration. The ratio in both cases, of course, has changed from year to year. Similar changes have occurred in the male-female ratio of homicide offenders, but in the case of homicide offenders the figures indicate a slight tendency to increase.

Conventional rates, the risk of becoming a homicide offender or victim, and the male-female ratio of offenders, victims, and participants have been utilized to study the change in murder patterns in Canada. The male-female ratio of offenders, victims, and participants are not significantly correlated with time ($r = -0.32, 0.25$, and -0.21 respectively). These changes are random occurrences. The changes that have occurred in the murder rate ($r = 0.89$), the homicide rate ($r = 0.84$), the homicide potential ($r = 0.91$), and the homicide risk ($r = 0.82$) are all significantly correlated with time. They all show an increase.

Table 5-2
Male-Female Ratio of Homicide Offenders and Victims (1961-1970)

Year	Offenders	Victims	Participants[a]
1961	7.85	1.50	2.85
1962	7.41	1.41	2.59
1963	12.06	1.34	3.01
1964	8.14	1.34	2.64
1965	8.74	1.41	2.77
1966	6.40	1.33	2.56
1967	7.96	1.23	2.38
1968	8.45	1.37	2.71
1969	5.95	1.92	3.01
1970	8.13	1.45	2.55

Source: Calculated from data published in the annual publication of the Dominion Bureau of Statistics: *Murder Statistics,* Table 11 and Table 14.

Note: Figures are males per female.

[a]Participants: Offenders and Victims combined.

The male-female ratio indicates no change in the incidence of murder, but, as this measure is not an established one, the increase indicated by the other measures permits only one conclusion—Verkko's contention of a relationship between the male-female ratio and the frequency of crimes against life could be incorrect.

The trend equations (Table 5-3) indicate an annual increase in both homicide potential and homicide risk of approximately 4.5 percent. These changes, it must be remembered, have occurred over the period 1961-1970, so that the increases noted began prior to the moratorium on the penalty of death. The increase in murder noticeable after the moratorium could consequently be only an extension of a trend that began earlier and independent of the changes in the penalty threatened. That such is the situation is the contention of Sellin[6] who found in his study of retentionist and abolitionist states in the United States a continuance of trends uninterrupted by changes in the punishment. In those states where homicide rates were decreasing, the decrease continued whether the penalty was changed or not. Similarly, rates continued to increase in those states in which rates were increasing. But can the continued increase or decrease in the homicide rates be assumed to be a continuation of prior established trends uninfluenced by punishment?

The influence that the suspension or abolition of the penalty of death exerts on the incidence of homicide can be only determined by the comparison

Table 5-3
Homicide Trends in Canada (1961-1970)

Murder Rate	$Y = e^{(0.1150 + 0.0690X)}$
Homicide Rate	$Y = e^{(0.2990 + 0.0460X)}$
Homicide Potential	$Y = e^{(1.9320 + 0.0460X)}$
Homicide Risk	$Y = e^{(1.9090 + 0.0460X)}$

Source: Calculated from the data presented in Tables 4-1 and 5-1.

Notes: Y in the Murder and Homicide Rate is homicides per 100,000 population and in the Homicide Potential and Homicide Risk chances in a million.
X is time in one year intervals with 1960 as zero.
e is the natural logarithm.

of the incidence in the same country at the same time with the penalty operant and nonoperant. Such a comparison is a physical impossibility. Faced with the problem of assessing the influence exerted by the control of malaria on population growth, Newman[7] found that the comparable situation could be artificially produced by using the before conditions to conceptually produce an after position in which the controlled factor was operant. It was his contention that had malaria not been controlled, population growth would have continued at a particular rate. Comparison of this growth—which he termed autonomous growth, computed theoretically under all prevailing conditions but without the control of malaria—with the actual growth, observed under all prevailing conditions including the control of malaria, gave the contribution made by the control of malaria to population growth. A similar model could be used in the study of the penalty of death. An after projection of the before trend gives an expected incidence in a situation similar to the after position but with the penalty of death supposedly operant. Comparison of this expected rate with the actually observed rate would reveal what influence the abolition or suspension of the death penalty had on the homicide problem. If a prior trend continued to operate, uninfluenced by the change in penalty, the expected rate would be no different from the actually observed one.

Using the trend of the homicide potential and homicide risk in Canada, 1961-1967, the expected homicide potential and the expected homicide risk in 1968 and 1969 can be computed. The projections showed the expected figures to be 9.96 and 10.00 for the homicide potential and 9.86 and 10.07 for the homicide risk in 1968 and 1969 respectively. The standard error of the estimate makes the maximum that could be expected for homicide potential 10.19 and 10.56 and for homicide risk 10.60 and 10.82 in 1968 and 1969 respectively. The actually observed homicide potential was 10.28 and 11.22 and the homicide risk 11.60 and 12.20, indicating an increase, since the moratorium on the penalty of death, over and above the expected attributable to social change alone.

The analysis of crime rates 1955-1966 led McDonald[8] to contend that the slight increase in murder rates noted in that period was more apparent than real. Using rates based on charges laid, McDonald has shown that while the murder rate showed a slight increase, there was no such increase discernible in the manslaughter rates. "If there was a real increase in murder," she contends, "we should expect to see an increase in manslaughter as well, since the dividing line between the two is not distinct." Taking the charges for murder and manslaughter together, she has shown that there has been no change in the combined rates: the estimated percent annual compound rate of change turned out to be zero. This analysis led her to conclude that the increase in the murder rate was due to cases of homicide that would have been dealt with as manslaughter prior to 1961—when murder became categorizable as capital and noncapital—that were dealt with as noncapital murder since 1961. In the present study, however, it has been found that the combined murder and manslaughter rates do show an increase (Table 5-4). The data utilized here differ from that used by McDonald first, in the figures used. In this study the homicide rates refer to all cases known to the police and not just to those cases in which the police have laid a charge, and the period studied has been longer.

Charge rates include the element of police activity that could conceivably alter the picture of commission on which the contention of an increase or decrease should rest. The superiority of crimes known to the police as a measure of criminality rests on Sellin's finding that the number of crimes tend to decrease

Table 5-4
Homicide Rates in Canada (1951-1970)

Year	Rate	Year	Rate
1951	2.04	1961	1.19
1952	1.18	1962	1.62
1953	1.19	1963	1.31
1954	1.14	1964	1.32
1955	0.76	1965	1.32
1956	0.79	1966	1.42
1957	0.85	1967	1.24
1958	0.74	1968	1.65
1959	0.70	1969	1.80
1960	0.88	1970	2.18

Source: A. Singh (1973) "Criminal Homicide and Culture Conflict in Canada" (Unpublished Master's Thesis. University of Ottawa). Reprinted with permission.

Note: Rates are per 100,000 population.

the further one gets from the event in terms of legal procedure.[9] A second element that makes the police statistics preferred, especially in trend studies, is the temporal variation of the proportion of cases that moves through the different stages of the legal process. In this connection it is perhaps pertinent to note that Singh has compared rates computed with the number of homicides known to the police and the number of persons convicted in Canada during the period 1951-1968. Not only were the rates different, the trends were too.[10]

The legal machinery put into motion by a crime comprises a number of processes—the investigation and solution of the case, the prosecution and trial of the offender, and the conviction and punishment or acquittal and release—each of which takes a variable time.[11] *Murder Statistics*[12] carry a series of tables designed to show the year's activity regarding murder and court proceedings. Updated each year, they permit a comparison of both the situation in each succeeding year and the progress that occurs in the years following. Table 5-5 shows the proportion of murder cases remaining unsolved in the year of commission and in the subsequent years. As the table shows, most murders are solved in the year of commission. This was the situation in 1963, 1965, and 1966. Some of the murders committed in 1964 were being solved as late as 1968. The limit for solving was reached by the end of the second year after commission for murder in 1967. An interesting feature of the data is that up to 1965 there is a decrease in the proportion of cases remaining unsolved and thereafter an increase.

Table 5-5
Proportion of Murders Unsolved (1961-1970)

Year of Commission	Years after Year of Commission					N
	0	*1*	*2*	*3*	*4*	*N*
1961				6.5	6.5	185
1962			10.6	10.6	10.6	217
1963		9.8	9.8	9.8	9.8	215
1964	9.2	9.3	7.3	6.9	6.4	218
1965	5.4	4.9	4.9	4.9	4.9	243
1966	6.4	6.4	6.4	6.4	6.4	240
1967	10.7	9.6	9.3	9.3		281
1968	14.0	13.7	12.8			314
1969	18.7	17.8				342
1970	15.6					430

Source: Calculated from data published in the annual publication of the Dominion Bureau of Statistics: *Murder Statistics*, Table 2.

Note: Figures are percentages of the total number of murders reported to have been committed in each year (*N*). The count is by victim.

One of the effects of the abolition or suspension of the penalty of death has been thought to be the greater ease in the solution of homicide cases. Not only, it has been contended, would the evidence required for conviction of a noncapital offence be less stringent than that required for conviction of a capital one, but also the public would be more willing to assist the police with information when the offence does not carry the death penalty.[13] The data presented here do not support this hypothesis of the greater ease of solution of homicide cases associated with the suspension of the penalty of death. The data actually suggest the reverse, but it must be remembered that the increase in the proportion of cases remaining unsolved began before the moratorium on the penalty.

The proportion of persons sent to trial who are convicted is shown in Table 5-6. As the years pass, the proportion convicted for any particular year tends to decrease. This, perhaps, results from the more straightforward cases where the evidence is strong, having been brought to court soon after commission. What cases are brought to court in later years, resulting in the reduction in conviction rates, are probably more complicated, where the evidence is

Table 5-6
Proportion Convicted of Persons Taken to Trial
(1961-1970)

Year of Commission	Years after Year of Commission				
	0	1	2	3	4
1961				61.7	59.4
1962			71.5	71.2	70.1
1963		66.7	66.5	65.1	65.1
1964	71.8	77.2	77.4	77.4	76.9
1965	80.3	81.1	78.9	78.9	79.2
1966	78.5	76.7	76.9	76.7	76.7
1967	87.5	81.2	80.8	80.5	
1968	81.1	80.2	76.3		
1969	82.5	79.5			
1970	75.8				

Source: Calculated from data presented in the annual publication of the Dominion Bureau of Statistics: *Murder Statistics,* Table 4.

Notes: Figures are percentages of the number of persons taken to trial for murders committed in a year up to the year of reckoning. Cases labelled "pending" have been excluded from the calculations.
  Conviction does not mean conviction of murder: it means conviction of a lesser offence as well.

not so strong. The proportion of persons sent to trial who are convicted has
shown an increase during the period of study, whether the data considered are
for the year of commission or for any year thereafter. The convictions, however,
have been for lesser offences rather than for murder. The proportion of those
convicted, who are convicted of murder, has shown a decline during the period
under consideration (Table 5-7) and, as in the case of solution of homicide cases,
the decreasing trend began prior to the moratorium on the penalty of death.
This finding too does not lend support to the belief that the abolition or suspension of the penalty of death makes the evidence required for conviction of
the "decapitalized" offence less stringent.

The changes that have occurred in the fate of homicide cases are subject to
two major interpretations. First, the nature of homicide in Canada is undergoing
change. It is undergoing a change that results not only in it being more difficult
to solve homicide cases, but also to obtain sufficient evidence—in those cases
that are solved—to secure a conviction of murder. The analysis of murders in
terms of the victim-offender relationship suggests a change in the nature of
murder. But this change in nature does not mean that the murders committed
in the more recent times are more difficult to solve. If the time taken to solve
a case is indicative of the ease of solution, the proportion of cases where investigation is not complete before the end of the year of commission should act as a

Table 5-7
Proportion Convicted of Murder (1961-1970)

Year of Commission	Years after Year of Commission				
	0	1	2	3	4
1961				36.7	36.7
1962			48.8	48.3	48.3
1963		44.2	44.8	45.4	45.4
1964	36.0	44.7	45.4	45.4	45.4
1965	39.6	42.2	42.2	42.2	43.2
1966	23.5	36.7	36.2	37.3	37.3
1967	21.3	33.8	33.3	32.8	
1968	18.3	22.7	23.8		
1969	28.2	33.5			
1970	37.8				

Source: Calculated from data published in the annual publication
of the Dominion Bureau of Statistics: *Murder Statistics,* Table 4.

Note: Figures are percentages of the number of persons convicted
of murder for homicides committed in a year up to the year of
reckoning.

reasonable measure of the ease of solution. There will, no doubt, always be a
number of cases that fall into this "pending" category because of the timing of
the incident, but as the homicides are distributed more or less equally over the
four seasons of the year, analysis will not be invalidated. The proportion of the
cases pending preliminary hearing at the end of the year of commission (Table
5-8) has varied from year to year, displaying an increasing trend. This variation
is not peculiar to any one type of homicide. It is seen in all types, though the
variation is more marked in the nondomestic types than in the domestic. The
differences, however, are not significant, forcing the rejection of the hypothesis linking the type of homicide with the ease of solution of the case.

The second explanation is that the police are less enthusiastic about solving
homicide cases. This decreased enthusiasm reduces the proportion of cases
that are solved. Further, as the cases that do get solved with this reduced enthusiasm are likely to be the relatively simple ones, in which the evidence is straightforward and clear, the proportion of persons taken to trial who are convicted
would increase. Variations in both the quantity and quality of the evidence
that is gathered could explain the reduction in the convictions of murder. Reduced enthusiasm on the part of the police is not an unreasonable explanation.
Compelled by workforce problems to apportion their investigative time according to the gravity of the offence, the moratorium on the penalty of death could

Table 5-8
**Proportion of Cases Pending Preliminary Hearing at the End of the Year of
Commission According to Type of Murder (1965-1970)**

	Type of Homicide			
Year	Domestic[a]	Criminal Act[b]	Nondomestic[c]	Total
1965	44.3[d]	28.1	44.8	41.9
1966	47.4	58.3	48.8	50.5
1967	42.9	54.2	37.4	41.5
1968	58.2	72.2	66.4	64.4
1969	54.2	60.9	52.7	54.5
1970	52.1	42.9	44.3	46.4

Source: Annual publication of the Dominion Bureau of Statistics: *Murder Statistics,*
Table 13.

[a]Domestic homicides are homicides where the victim is a member of the immediate or
extended family of the offender.

[b]Criminal Act homicides are ones committed during the commission of another crime.

[c]The nondomestic category contains all other homicides.

[d]Figures are proportions of cases falling into each category for that year.

possibly be viewed by the police as an indication of the reduction of the gravity of the offence of homicide in the eyes of the public, calling for the expenditure of less time and energy in the solution of homicide cases.

The reduced police enthusiasm explanation is only the mechanism through which a more basic explanation operates. This more basic explanation is that there is a change in the public attitude toward the offence. Conviction rates are conventionally thought to reflect police efficiency, but in reality they reflect public attitude. Whatever the offence may be, the conviction of an accused is not solely dependent on police efficiency. To counteract the efficiency or even the inefficiency of the police there is first the attitude of the victim and his or her relatives—an attitude that determines their desire to avenge the harm; second, there is the attitude of bystanders, onlookers, and witnesses who either consider what has happened none of their business or think that it is their duty to assist in seeing that justice is done; third, there is the attitude of the offender and relatives who are anxious to see that no punishment is inflicted though a crime be committed; fourth, there is the attitude of the judges, magistrates, and inquirers in the view that they take of the crime; and fifth, there is the attitude of the jury that influences the outcome in their determination as to whether a crime has been committed or not and if a crime has been committed what crime it was.[14] If the nature of murder, in terms of facility of solution, has not changed, the changes in the fate of homicide cases must necessarily reflect a change in the public attitude toward the offence.[15]

It has been contended that one way in which the deterrent effect of the death penalty operates is through the build-up in society over time of a peculiar feeling of abhorrence for the crime for which the penalty is threatened.[16] The findings in this study could be interpreted as tending to support this contention. The changes that have occurred in Canada—a decrease in the proportion of cases finally labelled murder independent of the change in the nature of the offence— could imply a change in the public concept of the gravity of the offence. However, the possibility of witting or unwitting artificial inflation must first be considered. The statistical data analyzed here indicate that the incidence of homicide in Canada has increased over and above what it normally should have, because of changes in social conditions, since the moratorium on the penalty of death. This increase, it must be pointed out, is in the number of cases labelled by the police as murder.

But other changes have also occurred. The sum total of these changes is a change in the proportion of cases that are finally labelled murder. Yet, when the murder rates are computed with actual convictions for murder (Table 5-9), there is no discernible change in rates. These rates do not correlate significantly with time ($r = 0.28$). Perhaps some other changes have occurred to account for the increase.

With the moratorium on the penalty of death, a system of legal aid has been introduced in Canada. This system brings with it better defences, longer periods

Table 5-9
Murder Rates: Based on Cases Known to Police
and Persons Convicted of Murder (1961-1970)

Year	Known to Police	Convicted
1961	1.2	0.4
1962	1.4	0.7
1963	1.4	0.6
1964	1.4	0.6
1965	1.5	0.7
1966	1.3	0.5
1967	1.6	0.5
1968	1.8	0.4
1969	1.9	0.6
1970	2.3	0.9

Source: Annual publication of the Dominion Bureau
of Statistics: *Murder Statistics.* Table 1, and Table 4.

Note: Rates are per 100,000 population 7 years and over.

of trial, more expense to government, better prosecutions to secure conviction, and a greater confidence in the ability of the legal system to see
that justice is done. In the absence of a system of legal aid, the onus
of seeing that justice is done falls on the prosecutors who could, with shorter
periods of trial, less expense to government, and less prepared and worse-
conducted prosecutions, secure the desired conviction. But then, they must
go home with the feeling that they have won the battle but lost the war. Under
these circumstances, a prosecution for murder, a conviction for which could,
perhaps, be easily obtained, would only be made when the prosecutor is fully
convinced that such a conviction serves well the ends of justice. When a legal
aid system exists, such precautions need not be exercised. There is no great
danger that an individual, accused of murder, would be unjustly convicted of
it. The defence attorney would see to it that such is not the case. The danger
now is that persons who should be convicted of murder may be not, especially
as the pressures of plea bargaining lead to the reduction of charges. Under
these circumstances the ends of justice are best served when there is an initial
indiscriminate labelling of all cases of unexplained death as murder. With this
orientation, the number of recorded murder cases would increase. So would
the proportion of cases remaining unsolved. The proportion of cases resulting
in a conviction of murder would decrease, and the proportion of cases resulting in a conviction of manslaughter would increase. This explanation suggests
the hypothesis that the observed increase in the incidence of murder in Canada
in recent times is more an artificial one created by alterations or changes in the
initial definitional procedure rather than an actual increase in the incidence.
The convergence, noted by the Dominion Bureau of Statistics, of Police murder

rates and Vital Statistics rates supports this view.[17] In this connection, it should perhaps be remembered that counts of murder result from the interaction of two forces – the commission of an act of homicide by an individual and the post facto evaluation of this act as murder. An observed increase in the counts need not necessarily mean an increase in the commission of the act.

Notes

1. See Chapter 4.

2. C. H. S. Jayewardene (1969) "The Measurement of Criminal Homicide." *Probation and Child Care Journal,* 7, 1-4.

3. M. E. Wolfgang (1958) *Patterns in Criminal Homicide* (Philadelphia: University of Pennsylvania Press).

4. V. Verkko (1951) *Homicides and Suicides in Finland and their Dependency on National Character* (Copenhagen: G. E. Gads Fortag).

5. C. H. S. Jayewardene (1960) "Criminal Homicide. A Study in Culture Conflict" (Unpublished Ph.D. Thesis. University of Pennsylvania).

6. Royal Commission on Capital Punishment (1954) *Evidence. 30th Day. Witness: Professor T. Sellin* (London: Her Majesty's Stationery Office).

7. P. Newman (1965) *Malaria Eradication and Population Growth* (Ann Arbor, Mich.: School of Public Health. University of Michigan).

8. L. McDonald (1969) "Crime and Punishment in Canada. A Statistical Test of the Conventional Wisdom." *Canad. Rev. Sociol. Anthropol.,* 6, 212-236; _____(1971) "Is the Crime Rate Increasing?" in C. L. Boydell, G. F. Grindstaff and P. C. Whitehead, *Critical Issues in Canadian Society* (Toronto: Holt, Rinehart and Winston of Canada, Ltd.) 467-478.

9. T. Sellin (1937) *Research Memorandum on Crime in the Depression* (New York: Social Science Research Council).

10. A. Singh (1973) "Criminal Homicide and Culture Conflict in Canada" (Unpublished M.A. Thesis. University of Ottawa).

11. C. H. S. Jayewardene and H. Ranasinghe (1961) *Criminal Homicide in the Southern Province* (Colombo, Sri Lanka: Colombo Apothecaries Co. Ltd).

12. Dominion Bureau of Statistics (1967) *Murder Statistics 1961-1965* (Ottawa: Queen's Printer); Dominion Bureau of Statistics (1967) *Murder Statistics 1966* (Ottawa: Queen's Printer); Dominion Bureau of Statistics (1968) *Murder Statistics 1967* (Ottawa: Queen's Printer); Dominion Bureau of Statistics (1969) *Murder Statistics 1968* (Ottawa: Queen's Printer); Dominion Bureau of Statistics (1970) *Murder Statistics 1969* (Ottawa: Queen's Printer); Dominion Bureau of Statistics (1971) *Murder Statistics 1970* (Ottawa: Queen's Printer).

13. Royal Commission on Capital Punishment (1954) *Report* (London: Her Majesty's Stationery Office).

14. C. H. S. Jayewardene "Criminal Homicide."
15. For further discussion see Chapter 3.
16. Royal Commission on Capital Punishment, *Report.*
17. See Chapter 4.

6 The Murder of Police Officers

Whenever an attempt is made to abolish the penalty of death, the question of police safety is raised. It is contended that abolition would increase the risk that police officers run in the performance of their duties.[1] This argument was most forcefully put by the Chief Constables Association of Canada in their brief to the Joint Committee of the Senate and the House of Commons on Capital Punishment[2] and has been reiterated since.[3] In contradistinction to this is the contention of the Chief of Police of Austria who thought that the police officer ran a greater risk of being killed during the apprehension of a criminal or the investigation of a crime if the criminals thought they would suffer death for the crime than if they knew they would not.[4] Up to the moment that the Chief Constables Association of Canada pleaded their point of view no attempt had been made to empirically test its veracity.[5] Since then, however, some attempts have been made. Empirical tests of this hypothesis post a multitude of problems – the main one being the nonavailability of relevant data. Ideally such tests should deal with assaults on police officers, whether the assaults resulted in death or not or, for that matter, in any injury at all; for, as Sellin[6] points out, whether the assault resulted in death or not could be just a matter of chance or the ready availability of medical aid. In the absence of data for such a study, criminologists have been forced to limit their studies to cases where death actually occurred.

One of the earliest studies in this connection was made by Campion.[7] He studied twenty four American police forces of which eighteen were in states retaining the death penalty and six in states that had abolished it. The study covered a period of fifty years and led to the conclusion that the data: "do not lend empirical support to the claim that the existence of the death penalty in the Statutes of a State provides a greater protection to the police than exists where the penalty had been abolished." Sellin[8] studied homicide of police in 183 cities in eleven states with capital punishment and 82 cites in six states without it over a period of twenty five years. His analysis of the data led him to contend that: "it is impossible to conclude that the states which had no death penalty had thereby made the policeman's lot more hazardous." This conclusion was based on the fact that the rate of police homicides in states with capital punishment was 1.3 per 100,000 of the total population and in states without it the rate was 1.2. Subsequently, he computed the risk of a police officer being killed in abolitionist and retentionist states using the number of police criminally killed during 1961-1963 and the number of police in

these states according to the 1960 census. The risk for the three years in
abolitionist states was 1.312 per 10,000 policemen and 1.328 in the bordering
retentionist states. He also points out that considering police who died in acci-
dents while on duty, the annual average risk of being killed on the job was
3.1 per 10,000 for police. In comparison the risk of being killed on the job
was 11 in the mining industry, 7.7 in contract construction, 6.5 in agriculture,
and 4.2 in transportation and public utilities.[9] Similar conclusions have been
reached by Carderelli,[10] but then he was using the same data as Sellin.

Other studies have also been conducted in the United States, all with
similar conclusions. A study conducted by Creamer and Robin[11] has shown
that most police officers have been killed with firearms and by persons with
a previous record. About a third of the deaths have occurred while crimes
were in progress and another third while a person was being arrested or transported. Only 6 percent of the killers were found to be insane. The analysis of
police officers killed and wounded in Chicago, 1919-1954, has shown that most
of them were killed in encounter and that in all but 26 of the 168 killings, the
killing occurred when police interfered with hold ups, were trying to arrest or
search a person, or were investigating some complaint[12] — all of which tends to
give the impression that the police officer's job is a highly hazardous one. However, Robin[13] contends that in the United States a police officer is about six
times as likely to kill than to be killed, while the probability of either event
occurring is extremely small. He also contends that police work is no more
hazardous than other occupations, though in these other occupations the
hazards are accidental with perhaps a large element of self-contribution, while
in police work they are not. Opposed to this is the view of Bristow[14] and
Creamer and Robin[15] that most police killed in the line of duty had reason to
believe that the persons they were dealing with were dangerous.

During the period 1961-1970 thirty-seven police officers have been killed
in Canada.[16] This is exclusive of two cases where the police were off duty
when they were killed. In one case, committed in 1961, the circumstances surrounding the killing related to the official duties of the police officer[17]; in the
other, committed in 1964, sufficient information is not available.[18] The
thirty-seven murders resulted from thirty-two separate incidents. In most cases
there was only one victim. Two police officers were killed in each of three
instances and three police officers in one. In two cases a civilian was killed in
addition to the police officers, and in three others, one or more officers
received serious injuries that did not result in death. In one of these cases one
officer lost an eye and another a lung. The maximum number of murders
during the period 1961-1970 occurred in 1962 when twelve police officers
were killed (Table 6-1). In 1963 there were no police killed. Two officers were
killed in 1961, 1964, and 1965; three in each of the years 1966, 1967, and
1970, and five in 1968 and 1969. The maximum number of killings occurred
in the Provinces of Quebec and Ontario. Twelve officers met with their death in

Table 6-1
Murder of Police Officers by Province and Year (1961-1970)

Province	1961	1962	1963	1964	1965	1966	1967	1968	1969	1970	Total
British Columbia		4			1						5
Saskatchewan						1				2	3
Alberta						1	1				2
Manitoba									1	1	2
Ontario		4			1	1	1	3	2		12
Quebec	2	4		1			1	2	2		12
New Brunswick											0
Prince Edward Island											0
Newfoundland				1							1
Nova Scotia											0
Yukon											0
Northwest Territories											0
Totals	2	12	0	2	2	3	3	5	5	3	37

Source: For 1961-1963: G. Favreau (1965) *Capital Punishment* (Ottawa: Queen's Printer). For 1964-1970: B. Grenier (1972) *Capital Punishment: New Material 1965-1972* (Ottawa: Queen's Printer).

Note: Figures are number of police officers killed.

each of these provinces. There were five killings in British Columbia, three in Saskatchewan, two each in Alberta and Manitoba, and one in Newfoundland. No police were killed in New Brunswick, Prince Edward Island, Yukon, the Northwest Territories, or Nova Scotia.

The most significant characteristic of the murder of police officers in Canada is the weapon that has been used. Killings have been done almost exclusively with firearms. Only in two cases were these not used. In both of these cases death was caused by a motor vehicle. In one the officer was the victim of a hit-and-run accident. In the other the dead officer was intentionally knocked down at a road block by the fugitive. In one case the fatal gun shot injury followed a stabbing. Also interesting is the fact that in five of the cases the firearm that was used was a police one. In one case it was the weapon issued to the offender, who utilized it to kill his superior who had suspended him from duties. In the other four cases the firearms were those carried by the victim and taken from him by the offender. These cases suggest the hypothesis of negligence on the part of the police. But the general pattern has not been a scuffle that ends with the shooting of the officer. When police were shot they were most frequently greeted with a volley of fire on arrival. They have almost always been taken by surprise.

Table 6-2 shows the circumstances surrounding the killings. In the majority of the cases the police officer was investigating a complaint. Most frequently this complaint referred to a crime of violence that had been or was being committed. Together with reports of disturbances, crimes of violence accounted for 35.2 percent of the police officers killed. Investigation of crimes against property, frauds, minor offences, and domestic squabbles also took their toll, but these account for 27 percent of those killed. A smaller proportion (18.9 percent) were killed when trying to apprehend an escaped convict or a suspect. In most of these cases, contrary to expectation, the death did not result from a shoot-out between the police and the criminal. Transportation of insane people to a mental hospital and revenge each accounted for 8.1 percent of the killings.

Though the killing of a police officer is described in law as constituting capital murder, all these cases did not end in the conviction of the individuals concerned of this offence. Of the thirty-nine persons responsible for the killing of police officers, ten had had "justice" meted out summarily — three had been killed by other police officers in the course of the incident, and seven had committed suicide. Eight were found not guilty by reason of insanity. Of the remaining twenty-one, eight were found guilty of capital murder, seven of noncapital murder, five of manslaughter, and one of assault. (See Table 6-3.) Thus the number of people who kill police who are acting in the course of duty, with malice aforethought, and consequently liable to suffer death, are extremely few.

The moratorium of 1967 excluded the killing of police acting in the course

Table 6-2

Circumstances Surrounding the Killing of Police Officers (1961-1970)

	1961	1962	1963	1964	1965	1966	1967	1968	1969	1970	Total
Investigation of											
Crimes of violence		4			1		1	2		2	10
Disturbances						1	1		1		3
Robberies		2						2	1		5
Frauds		1									1
Minor offences		1							1		2
Domestic squabbles						1			1		2
Apprehension of											
Suspects		1					1			1	3
Escaped convicts		1		1				1	1		4
Service of summons				1							1
Transport of Insane		1			1	1					3
Revenge	2	1									3
Total	2	12		2	2	3	3	5	5	3	37

Source: For 1961-1963: G. Favreau (1965) *Capital Punishment* (Ottawa: Queen's Printer). For 1964-1970: B. Grenier (1972) *Capital Punishment: New Material 1965-1972* (Ottawa: Queen's Printer).

Note: Figures refer to police officers killed.

Table 6-3
Fate of Offender in Cases of Police Killings (1961-1970)

| | Circumstances Surrounding Killing | | | | | | | | | | | |
Fate	A	B	C	D	E	F	G	H	I	J	K	Total
Committed Suicide	2					1		1		1	2	7
Killed by Police	1						1	1				3
Declared Insane	2		1			1			1	2	1	8
Convicted of:												
Capital murder	1	1	2	1			2	1				8
Noncapital murder		1	5		1							7
Manslaughter			4					1				5
Assault			1									1
Total	6	2	13	1	1	2	3	4	1	3	3	39
Case Unsolved		1				1						2

A: Investigation of Crimes of Violence
B: Investigation of Disturbances
C: Investigation of Robberies
D: Investigation of Frauds
E: Investigation of Minor Offences
F: Investigation of Domestic Squabbles
G: Apprehension of Suspects
H: Apprehension of Escaped Convicts
I: Service of Summons
J: Transport of Insane
K: Revenge

Source: For 1961-1963: G. Favreau (1965) *Capital Punishment* (Ottawa: Queen's Printer). For 1964-1970: B. Grenier (1972) *Capital Punishment: New Material 1965-1970* (Ottawa: Queen's Printer).

of duty, as if in acceptance of the police argument that the absence of the peanlty of death from the statutes would increase the risk run by a police officer in the maintenance of law and order. Yet, each time a police officer gets killed in Canada, the moratorium has been cited by the police as the cause of this undesirable state of affairs. The police contention, however, is not totally irrational. Even before the moratorium those condemned to death for the murder of a police officer have had their sentences commuted, so that in effect the murder of an officer was noncapital murder. However, the contention that the moratorium contributed to the risk of police has no factual support. Table 6-4 shows the number of persons convicted of capital

Table 6-4
Capital Murders Involving Police Officers (1941-1970)

Year	Convicted	Executed	Year	Convicted	Executed
1941	1	0	1956	0	0
1942	0	0	1957	3	1
1943	0	0	1958	0	0
1944	1	0	1959	1	1
1945	0	0	1960	0	0
1946	1	1	1961	0	0
1947	1	1	1962	3	1
1948	0	0	1963	0	0
1949	3	3	1964	1	0
1950	1	1	1965	0	0
1951	0	0	1966	0	0
1952	2	2	1967	1	0
1953	0	0	1968	0	0
1954	0	0	1969	1	0
1955	0	0	1970	1	0

Source: For 1941-1963: G. Favreau (1965) *Capital Punishment* (Ottawa: Queen's Printer). For 1964-1970: B. Grenier (1972) *Capital Punishment. New Material 1965-1970* (Ottawa: Queen's Printer).

murder for the killing of a police officer and the number executed during the period 1941-1970. The last execution was in 1962. During the seven-year period 1964-1970, when no one was executed and when a killer of a police officer could reasonably expect to have his or her life spared, there were four capital murders. During the seven-year period 1956-1962, when persons convicted of capital murder were executed, there were a total of seven capital murders where police officers were victims. It could perhaps be argued that during this period there was no certainty of execution, for only three of seven convicted were executed. During the seven-year period 1948-1954 every single person convicted of capital murder for the killing of an officer was executed. During this period there were six such cases.

Though the executions of killers of police officers are dependent on their being convicted of capital murder, the argument that the absence of the death penalty increases the risk of a police officer implies that all killing of officers, no matter what the post facto designation may be, would be much less with the death penalty in the statutes than with it out. According to this argument it is not just the killings that end in a conviction of murder that must be considered but all killing of police on duty. These figures are given in the Dominion Bureau of Statistics publication *Police Administration Statistics*. These publications also give the number of police personnel. With these sets of figures it is possible to compute an "on-the-job risk of death" for

police.[a] This risk for the period 1963-1971[b] is shown in Table 6-5. For the
total period the average annual risk is 2.82 per 10,000. The risk in the Yukon
(72.60) is much higher than that in other provinces. But this is due to the
smallness of the police force in this territory and four accidental deaths that
occurred in 1963. It is, however, only in Quebec and Ontario that the police
are killed accidentally or by criminal intent every year. The risk in these two
provinces has varied from year to year, but these changes do not represent
any trend. Correlation with time shows a slight but statistically insignificant
($r = 0.26$) increase in Quebec, a slight but statistically insignificant ($r = -0.63$)
decrease in Ontario, and a slight but statistically insignificant ($r = -0.64$)
decrease in all Canada.

The data on police killings in Canada do not support the hypothesis that
the absence of the death penalty from the statutes increases the risk of the
police officer. The changes in the number killed by criminal action does not
support it. The changes in the number of convictions of capital murder for the
killing of police also do not support it. Nor do the changes in the "on-the-job
risk of death" support the hypothesis. Police do run a risk of being killed. The
variations of this risk from year to year, however, indicate that it is no more
than a to-be-expected occupational risk. Analysis of police killings in the
United States has led to the contention that like most other occupational
risks, its actualization is promoted by the negligence of the worker and that the
adoption of proper precautionary measures would minimize it. The common
pattern of police killings in Canada — the police officer is summoned to a
trouble spot and greeted on arrival by a volley of fire — does not support this
hypothesis. This, however, does not mean that some of the police killings
could not have been prevented. In this connection it is pertinent to note that
four of the police killed were killed with the firearm that they themselves
carried. The police who were killed while transporting insane individuals to a
mental hospital could perhaps have escaped death if the possibility of an
insane man becoming violent had been appreciated and precautions taken. The
mere handcuffing of the individual would have been sufficient. Details of cases
gleaned from newspaper reports[19] indicate that there are other cases where the
death could be attributed to some form of foolhardy or negligent behaviour on
the part of the police. Thus, one police officer, listed as being killed while
apprehending a suspect, was killed by a man who had driven to the police
station on being requested to do so by a police officer. While being questioned
at the police station, he had run out and escaped in his own car. Subsequent

---

[a]Total number of police killed while on duty — both accidentally and by criminal intent
divided by the total number of police personnel and expressed in terms of per 10,000
police.

[b]Comparable data are not available for the computation of the risk prior to 1963. The
number of police deaths are available but not the total number of police personnel.

Table 6-5
On-the-Job Risk of Death for Police Officers (1963-1971)

	1963	1964	1965	1966	1967	1968	1969	1970	1971	Average
Newfoundland		20.24								1.87
Prince Edward Island										
Nova Scotia	11.42						8.62			2.12
New Brunswick						12.20			10.28	2.97
Quebec	2.42	2.22	3.15	1.69	3.97	5.54	3.00	1.40	3.99	3.10
Ontario	6.15	2.93	10.71	3.78	1.41	4.71	1.94	1.23	0.59	2.45
Manitoba		8.58					5.86	11.14	4.38	3.63
Saskatchewan				14.13			5.98	11.60		3.89
Alberta	5.30	5.26			10.41					2.15
British Columbia		7.95	3.85	3.24				2.46	2.24	2.33
Yukon	727.3									72.60
Northwest Territories										
Total (Canada)	5.23	3.82	1.70	3.00	2.57	3.74	2.38	2.00	2.13	2.82

Source: Calculated from data in Dominion Bureau of Statistics: *Police Administration Statistics*, Tables 4 and 11 (Ottawa: Queen's Printer).

Note: Figures are risks per 100,000 police personnel.

Trend line equations: Ontario $Y = 7.36 - 0.73X$ ($r = -0.63$) Quebec $Y = 2.43 + 0.12X$ ($r = -0.26$) Canada $Y = 4.27 - 0.26X$ ($r = -0.64$) Y is the risk and X is in one year intervals with 1962 as 0.

attempts to apprehend him resulted in a shoot-out in which a police officer and the suspect were killed. The suspect was using a rifle that had been in his car. Had the car been examined and the rifle removed, or had the car been locked at the police station, this officer's death may not have resulted. Again one officer listed as being killed while investigating a robbery had rushed into a bank where he had seen a hold up in progress and demanded the armed robbers to give themselves up. Had he been slower to enter, first summoning help, he may not have been killed. The post facto analysis of the circumstances surrounding the cases suggests that the police officer's death could have perhaps been prevented had sufficient precautionary measures been taken by the police in about 20 percent of the cases.

Notes

1. R. J. Goetz (1961) "Should Ohio Abolish Capital Punishment?" *Cleveland Marshall Law Rev.*, 10, 365-377.

2. Joint Committee of the Senate and the House of Commons on Capital and Corporal Punishment and Lotteries (1956) *Report* (Ottawa: Queen's Printer).

3. C. H. S. Jayewardene (1972) "The Canadian Movement Against the Penalty of Death." *Canad. Jour. Criminol. Correct.*, 14, 377-391.

4. Joint Committee of the Senate and the House of Commons on Capital and Corporal Punishment and Lotteries (1955) *Minutes of Proceedings and Evidence. Appendix F.* (Ottawa: Queen's Printer).

5. T. Sellin (1959) *The Death Penalty* (Philadelphia: The American Law Institute).

6. Sellin, *Death Penalty.*

7. D. Campion (1956) "The State Police and the Death Penalty." *Congressional Record*, March 6, A 2076-2080. Also in Joint Committee of the Senate and the House of Commons on Capital and Corporal Punishment and Lotteries, *Minutes of Proceedings.*

8. Sellin *Death Penalty.*

9. T. Sellin (1967) "The Death Penalty and Police Safety," in T. Sellin, *Capital Punishment* (New York: Harper and Row) 138-153.

10. A. P. Carderelli (1968) "An Analysis of Police Killed by Criminal Action. 1961-1963." *Jour. Crim. Law Criminol.*, 59, 447-453.

11. S. J. Creamer and G. Robin (1970) "Assaults on Police," in S. Chapman, *Police Patrol Reader* (Springfield, Ill. C. C. Thomas) 485-494.

12. Sellin *Death Penalty.*

13. G. D. Robin (1963) "Justifiable Homicide by Police Officers." *Jour. Crim. Law Criminol.*, 54, 225-231; _____ (1967) "Justifiable Homicide by Police Officers," in M. E. Wolfgang: *Studies in Homicide* (New York: Harper and Row) 88-100.

14. A. C. Bristow (1963) "Police Officers Shootings. A Tactical Evaluation." *Jour. Crim. Law Criminol.*, 54, 93-95.

15. Creamer and Robin, "Assaults on Police."

16. The information here has been obtained from: G. Favreau (1965) *Capital Punishment* (Ottawa: Queen's Printer); B. Grenier (1972) *Capital Punishment: New Material 1965-1972* (Ottawa: Queen's Printer).

17. Favreau, *Capital Punishment.*

18. Grenier, *Capital Punishment: New Material.*

19. E. Hughes (1972) "Analysis of Canadian Police Homicide" (Unpublished manuscript. University of Ottawa).

7 Public Opinion

Whenever governments in Canada have introduced legislation to amend the criminal code in respect to the penalty of death, members of Parliament have been allowed a free vote. They have been permitted to vote according to their conscience rather than to tow the party line represented in the bill. In January 1973, when legislation was introduced to extend the moratorium on Capital Punishment for an additional five-year period, the Association of Chiefs of Police suggested that members of Parliament should exercise this free vote by voting not according to their conscience but according to the desires of the people they represent. In a democratic form of government, members of Parliament (it was the contention of the Police Chiefs) were essentially the voice of the people, and, as such, especially in matters of importance such as capital punishment, their vote should be the expression not of their views of right and wrong but of the desires of the people they represent.[1] Whatever the form of government may be, legislation should seek to establish a just society where the resultant social structure provides the maximum benefit for the maximum number of people. When, however, the maximum benefit and the maximum number of people are to be assessed in objective rather than subjective terms, objectivity is frequently sought to be established, in the absence of a measure for assessment, by consideration of the desires of the people, whether these desires have a rational or emotional base.

When the necessity to answer anew the question on capital punishment became imminent, mass media in Canada attempted to whip up public interest in the subject. The fact was brought to the notice of the public in newscasts associated with a "special feature" exposition on the subject. In addition to these special feature expositions both radio and television have broadcast the views of "knowledgeable" Canadians on the subject. These persons were mainly members of Parliament, lawyers, and sociology professors. Though no attempt was made to convey the impression that they reflected public opinion, their input was considered desirable and even sufficient to provide the public with the necessary data base to form an informed opinion. Like the radio and television, the newspapers too have carried feature articles.[2] But what they have done on this occasion looks like a half-hearted attempt to make the people feel that they too are interested. In this connection, it is perhaps interesting to note that on prior occasions, when there existed a prospect that the question of capital punishment would be raised, the newspapers carried a number of editorials and feature articles on the subject.[3] They usually carried a series of

articles that presented both sides of the picture, though they declared themselves committed to the one side or other.[4] On this occasion too, newspapers
have editorialized[5] but not with the same fervour as before.

Public interest in the subject at this time also did not appear to be too
enthusiastic. Occasional letters to the editor appeared in the press in favor of
both retention[6] and abolition,[7] but these letters are like cries in the wilderness
evoking little or no response from others. Letters to the editor and the organization of, and participation in, public meetings—while indicating public interest—
do not provide too reliable a measure of public opinion and attitude. The
attitude of the public could perhaps best be determined through a public
opinion poll. In one letter to the newspapers it has been suggested that future
legislation on capital punishment should be guided by the results of a referendum.[8] An attempt to do precisely this was unsuccessfully made in 1960 when
Yvon Dupuis, member for St. Jean-Iberville-Napierville, introduced in Parliament
Bill No. C-49 to provide for a poll of public opinion on capital punishment.
Though no official public opinion poll on capital punishment has been taken in
Canada, private polls have and the results of these, it is claimed, have been taken
into consideration by members of Parliament in their decision to vote on a bill
the one way or the other.[9]

Recent public opinion polls, it has been claimed, indicate a strong pro-
retentionist attitude. The extent to which this interpretation is correct can be
ascertained only by analyzing what exactly the polling constituted. One poll
whose results are so interpreted is that conducted by Raymond Rock, sitting
member from the Quebec riding of Lachine. He sent out 31,354 questionnaires
to his constituents in the municipalities of Lachine, Dorval, and Pointe Claire
asking them, inter alia, whether they favoured the abolition of the penalty of
death. By January 20, 1972, he had received 3700 replies (a response of 12 percent) of which 3583 had answered the question on capital punishment. Of
these 2814 (76 percent) had favoured retention.[10] All other polls[11] have
followed a more or less similar format. A large number of questionnaires are
sent out. A small proportion are returned. The responses received are then
analyzed, and the results are interpreted as if the sample responding comprised
a random sample of the population. In most of these polls a large majority of
those responding did seem to favour retention. Yet the results cannot be interpreted as indicating the overwhelming support for retention that is frequently
claimed. All that they show is that the large proportion of the public do not
consider the issue sufficiently important to be bothered with it.

A Gallup Poll conducted by the Canadian Institute of Public Opinion, it is
claimed, also shows an overwhelming desire for restoration of the penalty. This
poll had revealed that 66 percent of Canadians wanted the death penalty rein-
stated while 30 percent did not. A small 4 percent appeared uninterested.[12]
The appellation Gallup Poll carries the connotation of conductance with careful
attention to the statistical rules and analysis with due consideration to them so

as to ensure that the published answers represent a more or less accurate picture of the situation. In accepting these results, however, it must be realized that the question was worded: "The suspension of the penalty of death comes to an end this year. Do you want it brought back?" While a negative answer means total abolition (a step further from the present situation), a positive answer could mean death in all cases of murder or only in certain cases. The former implies a return to the premoratorium situation and the latter a continuation of the present one. This distinction has seldom been appreciated. Even when information necessary for such a distinction is obtained, the results have been reported in the dichotomous retention-abolition terms by lumping in the former category all those who were not in favour of total abolition. Thus it was claimed that 80.2 percent demanded the restoration of the death penalty,[13] because 34.9 percent wanted the penalty as punishment for all cases, and 45.3 percent wanted it to be the punishment in certain cases.[14] The survey canvassed the opinion of 316 persons in Montreal. It showed that 18 percent of these people (20 percent of the men and 15.9 percent of the women) wanted total abolition of the penalty, 45.3 percent of the people (41.3 percent of the men and 49.7 percent of the women) were for its restricted use—it being threatened as punishment only in certain cases of murder. Those who wanted the death penalty restored for all cases of murder constituted 34.9 percent of the people (36.9 percent of the males and 32.5 percent of the females).[15]

A second contention that is made about public opinion is that there is a decrease in the public support for abolition.[16] The basis for this contention is that in 1953 public opinion polls revealed a 70 percent support for retention. Since then, until very recently, this proportion averaged 53 percent. The present support is 66 percent—a distinct increase. Considering the support for abolition, those who feel that the trend in public opinion is for retention point out that 22 percent of Canadians supported abolition in 1943, 33 percent in 1958, 41 percent in 1960, and 35 percent in 1965. The 22 percent in support of abolition in present-day surveys are seen as indicating a waning support for abolition since 1961, when the peak of 41 percent was reached.[17] A possible interpretation of these findings, not considered, is an increasing disinterest in the subject. It may well be that the Canadian public is beginning to feel that the fate of the penalty of death is a destiny they cannot help to fashion.

The most scientific attempt to assess public attitude toward the penalty of death was made by Boydell and Grindstaff in their assessment of the public opinion on legal sanctions.[18] They asked people what they considered should be the most frequent, the minimum, and the maximum punishment for a number of crimes of which capital murder and noncapital murder were two. They received a 45 percent return. Execution was considered the desired maximum punishment for capital murder by 70 percent and for noncapital murder by 51 percent. It was considered the desired minimum punishment for capital murder by 21 percent and for noncapital murder by 13 percent. A

response that execution should be the minimum punishment indicates a firm
conviction that the death penalty should be inflicted for that crime whatever
the circumstances may be. A response that execution should not be the maximum punishment likewise indicates a firm conviction that the penalty of death
should not be inflicted for that crime whatever the circumstances may be.
These responses represent basic immutable convictions. An undecided response,
or no response, on the other hand, represent nonbasic convictions where the one
reaction (execution) is considered as good as the other (nonexecution). The 30
percent who did not consider execution the desired maximum punishment
for even capital murder indicates a 13.5 percent support for total abolition,
considering the fact that the response was only 45 percent. Similarly support
for total restoration of the penalty is only 5.9 percent—only 13 percent of the
45 percent responding considered it the desireable minimum for noncapital
murder. Considering the fact that 55 percent of the population do not have
strong views on the subject, the results of the poll indicate total abolition
unopposed by 68.5 percent of the population, while the restoration of the premoratorium status is unopposed by only 60.9 percent.

In the United States Gallup polls have, at intervals, asked a representative
sample of the U.S. population whether they were in favor of the death penalty
for persons convicted of murder. In 1953, 68 percent of those who were
polled answered yes. Since then there has been a steady decline in the proportion. In 1960, it was 52 percent; in 1965, 45 percent and in 1966, 42 percent.[19]
A Roper poll taken in the United States in 1958, however, indicated that 42
percent of the people favored execution rather than life imprisonment of persons
convicted of murder. At this poll 50 percent were found to be against the
death penalty and 8 percent to have no opinion.[20] The difference could perhaps
be attributed to characteristics of the samples polled, for in all these polls it has
been found that a much larger proportion of the poor and nonwhite than the
rich or white people were against the penalty of death. Thus in the Roper poll
53 percent of the lowest-income groups were against the death penalty as
compared with 42 percent of the highest-income groups. Of the blacks inter-
viewed, 78 percent were opposed.[21] In the Gallup polls combined, 45 percent
of white males and 58 percent of white females favored abolition of the death
penalty, while 65 percent of black males and 69 percent of black females did
so.[22] The preferences of the different ethnic groups in Canada is unknown, but
occupational groups have declared themselves on one side or the other.

Jayewardene and Singh have conducted a public opinion poll on the penalty
of death among Ottawa residents. To avoid the possible effect of sample com-
position on the result, they sent out a questionnaire to 2000 persons chosen
from voter's lists on a multistage random process. To avoid possible errors from
the dichotomous division of for and against, they sought responses regarding the
propriety of the penalty for (1) all killing, (2) unintentional and accidental
killing, (3) killing in domestic settings, and (4) killing of police and prison

guards. The responses to these questions permitted thirty two possible combinations, which were divided into the five groups: (1) total abolitionists, (2) near-total abolitionists, (3) partial abolitionists/retentionists, (4) near-total retentionists, and (5) total retentionists. They had a response rate of 37.1 percent, and their data showed their sample to be divided 20.1 percent total abolitionists, 23.7 percent near-total abolitionists, 6.4 percent partial abolitionists/retentionists, 45.7 percent near-total retentionists, and 4.1 percent total retentionists. As their sample was not representative of the Ottawa population educationwise, a correction was made and the results interpreted in terms of "those not against" and "those definitely for." The study showed 17.4 percent to be definitely for total abolition, 25.4 percent for death for the killing of peace officers with 42.8 percent not against, 45.6 percent for death for all murder with 49.7 percent not against, and 4.1 percent for the use of the penalty for all killings.[23]

The Canadian Correctional Chaplains' Association contends that all the Christian Churches in Canada are against the penalty of death. In 1966, the Anglican Church of Canada, the Baptist Convention of Ontario and Quebec, the Religious Society of Friends, the Lutheran Church of America—Canadian Chapter, and the United Church of Canada all made official statements opposing capital punishment. The Presbyterian Church in Canada supported capital punishment, but since then it has officially changed its position and is now against it.[24] The statements made by the Churches have not been the rash utterances of emotionalism. They stem from prolonged and profound consideration. The United Church of Canada, for example, decided at its Seventeenth General Council in 1956 that capital punishment was contrary to the spirit and teaching of Christ, but it did not recommend abolition. Such a step, it was contended, should be taken only when an appropriate alternative was found. A committee appointed to investigate deliberated four years before they concluded that life imprisonment was the appropriate alternative.[25] It was only after this that the Church declared itself against capital punishment.

The one occupational group that has persistently opposed the abolition of the penalty is the police. The Canadian Association of Chiefs of Police in a brief submitted to the Joint Committee of the Senate and the House of Commons on Capital Punishment, Corporal Punishment and Lotteries urged the retention of capital punishment. Their main arguments were that the penalty was a deterrent and that its abolition would increase the risk of death run by police.[26] In 1964 they addressed a letter to the Prime Minister protesting against the policy of commuting death sentences. A copy of this letter and a copy of their brief was sent by them in 1965 to all members of Parliament, contending that "the present state of lawlessness in the country" was due to the granting of clemency to vicious murderers.[27] What exactly the police feel on the subject is revealed by the resolutions recently passed by the Ontario

Police Association. In 1971 they resolved to request the federal government to limit the exercise of the Royal Prerogative of Mercy to cases where there was a jury recommendation for one.[28] In 1972 they resolved to ask the federal government to retain the death penalty as the ultimate punishment for all persons convicted of murder—capital and noncapital.[29] At this meeting Sidney Brown, the Association Chairman, asked member associations to compile capital punishment views of candidates in the next federal election, so that they could have some idea as to how members of the House of Commons would vote when the issue came up.[30] This request is interesting becase of the contention of the Police Chiefs in their letter to members of Parliament that the abolitionists had organized themselves to press for their objectives: "while the average good citizen essentially a retentionist was too busy with his own problems to make his views known."[31] It is not only police officers who have campaigned for the death penalty, the wives of police have banded themselves into a group to demand the reestablishment of the death penalty for all murderers and the loss of Cabinet power to commute death sentences except when courts recommend mercy and life imprisonment as an alternative to the death sentence.[32]

The Canadian Bar Association had at its summer convention of 1971 resolved to request the government to extend the moratorium on capital punishment. The legal profession has not always been for the liberalization of punishment. Influenced considerably perhaps by Beccarian philosophy, members of the legal profession have made statements that underscore the belief that the incidence of crime was solely determined by the severity of the punishment threatened for it. All lawyers, however, have not displayed this disposition. There have been many who have campaigned vigorously for the abolition of the death penalty, but the majority of them have thought that the penalty did serve an important function.

In 1954, when the Minister of Justice appointed a Parliamentary Committee to inquire into the penalty of death for murder in Canada, the Ontario members of the Canadian Bar Association devoted a session of its mid-winter meeting to debate capital punishment. To assist its members to arrive at a conclusion on that important issue, the Bar Association invited several men and women, representatives of the Bench, the Bar, the Church, the medical profession, and the press, to express their views. Those for and against the penalty were more or less equally matched. The debate, however, was not even an academic exercise. After these opinions were expressed, the debate was adjourned without a vote being taken. This procedure was adopted, it was claimed, because of the lack of adequate time for further and fuller discussion.[33]

The Report of the Joint Committee on Capital Punishment was reviewed in the *Canadian Bar Review* by P. J. O. Hearn.[34] Approving the recommendation of the Committee to retain the penalty of death, he concludes:

Human respect and public tradition are perhaps the most potent forces making for obedience to law. The committee has recognized this and has based its various proposals upon a thorough sociological study of the Canadian people within the scope of its inquiries and has developed solutions that correspond to the Nation's present needs and outlook.

Reflecting a similar sentiment is an article written by Reverend E. L. H. Taylor and published in the Bar Association's other journal—*The Canadian Bar Journal*.[35] Taylor's article was prompted by what he calls the growing feeling, especially among Canadian lawyers, against the penalty of death. Influenced and perturbed by the government's generous exercise of the Royal Prerogative of Mercy and the public's letters to the editor (published in the *Globe and Mail* during the period April 18th through April 28th), he points out that the abolition of capital punishment would mean the destruction of the very foundation of Western civilization—a movement from the sacred to the secular. Opposing these sentiments was J. D. Morton[36] and opposing him was W. B. Hagarty,[37] both lawyers of repute. In this connection it is perhaps pertinent to note that the 1961 bill to define murder as capital and noncapital was most vociferously objected to by lawyers, some on the belief that the wording did not do what the bill intended and others on the contention that what the bill did was insufficient,[38] but with both wanting a bill nearer abolition.

There have been other groups that have declared themselves for, or against, the penalty of death, and these declarations have been used by members of Parliament to support their position in the numerous Parliamentary debates on the subject. Yet there appears to have been a reluctance on the part of groups to debate the question. The reluctance may have been due to the strength of feeling on the subject, which, when expressed in a debate, was likely to destroy the unity of the group. This view has been expressed by J. A. Edmison in his evidence before the Joint Committee of the Senate and the House of Commons on Capital Punishment, Corporal Punishment and Lotteries. Speaking specifically of Prisoners' Aid Societies, he contended that many a society had been split right down the middle by the death penalty debate and that, whenever he participated in setting up a John Howard Society in a Canadian community, he advised the charter members to stay clear of this contentious subject.[39]

In the debate against capital punishment, who the people are who align themselves on either side is a question that has not been answered. Some studies have attempted to reveal their socioeconomic and demographic characteristics. Their personality characteristics have been left unexplored. It has, however, been claimed that the abolitionists are essentially sentimentalists who, through a misguided sense of humanity, seek to prevent evil-doers from receiving their just punishment. The retentionists, on the other hand, the contention goes, are rationalists seeking to utilize the most efficient means, distasteful though they may be, to protect society. This was the orientation with which Gowers accepted his task as Chairman of the Royal Commission on Capital Punishment. Several years of study, however, showed him that the situation was just the reverse. The abolitionists had all the arguments on their side, while the retentionists had their opinion fashioned by emotion.[40] Recently an attempt has been made by Dandurand and Fontaine[41] to test this hypothesis. Using Sellin's categorization of arguments as dogmatic and utilitarian[42] and Rokeach's conceptualization of minds as open and closed,[43] they attempted to determine whether it was the abolitionists or retentionists that were characterized by emotionality. They asked ninety four students at the University of Ottawa what their position was on capital punishment and the reasons for the views they held. At the same time they administered to them the E version of Rockeach's Dogmatism Scale.[44] The data they gathered thus led them to the conclusion that dogmatic arguments were used equally frequently by abolitionists and retentionists and that open-mindedness and closed-mindedness characterized neither the abolitionists nor retentionists on the one hand and neither those who used dogmatic reasons nor utilitarian reasons on the other.

Jayewardene and Singh, as a part of their study on the public opinion on the death penalty, attempted to determine whether the stand a person took was fashioned by his or her informational base. With reference to the situation in Canada they contended that a person would have rational justification for supporting the penalty of death if after the moratorium he or she personally knew more people who had been killed, believed that more people had been killed, and thought the moratorium endangered life. Their data revealed that less than 10 percent showed any logical consistency. Over 80 percent, whether abolitionists or retentionists, held views on the punishment that were not consistent with the views they held on the effect of abolition.[45]

Notes

1. *Ottawa Journal* (1973) January 20th.

2. *Edmonton Journal* (1972) January 29th; *Ottawa Citizen* (1971) November 8th, December 18th; *Ottawa Journal* (1971) March 17th; *Ottawa Journal* (1972) January 4th; *Truro Daily News* (1972) January 17th.

3. *Calgary Herald* (1967) April 22nd; *Financial Post* (1946) October 12th; *Globe and Mail* (1948) April 27th; *L'Action* (1967) October 23rd; *Ottawa Citizen* (1965) June 25th; *Ottawa Citizen* (1966) March 7th; *Ottawa Citizen* (1967) November 8th; *Telegram* (1946) May 17th; *The Star* (1946) July 13th; *The Star* (1953) January 5th.

4. For example, see Ottawa Citizen (1961) *Capital Punishment. A Collection of News, Views and Comments as they appeared during January 1960 in the pages of the Ottawa Citizen* (Ottawa: Ottawa Citizen).

5. *Ottawa Citizen* (1973) January 22nd.

6. *Globe and Mail* (1971) April 21st, April 29th; *The Gazette* (1971) October 15th; *The Gazette* (1972) October 18th.

7. *Globe and Mail* (1971) April 24th, April 29th; *Le Devoir* (1971) October 20th.

8. *Montreal Star* (1972) February 1st.

9. Canada (1967) *Debates: House of Commons.* 27th Parliament, 2nd Session. 4077, 4098, 4103-4118, 4142-4164, 4244-4266, 4274-4293, 4311-4320, 4336-4357, 4365-4381, 4570-4585, 4604-4621, 4629-4644, 4846-4861, 4879-4893.

10. *The Gazette* (1972) February 2nd.

11. *Ottawa Citizen* (1973) March 17th.

12. *Montreal Star* (1972) February 2nd.

13. *The Gazette* (1971) August 17th.

14. *La Presse* (1971) August 16th.

15. *Sonopresse Survey* (1971) August 14th.

16. *Montreal Star* (1972) February 2nd.

17. *Sonopresse Survey* (1971) August 14th.

18. C. L. Boydell and C. F. Grindstaff (1972) "Public Attitude and Legal Sanctions," in C. L. Boydell, C. F. Grindstaff, and P. C. Whitehead: *Deviant Behaviour and Societal Reaction* (Toronto: Holt, Rinehart and Winston) 162-184.

19. H. Ziesel (1968) *Some Data on Jury Attitudes toward Capital Punishment* (Chicago: University of Chicago. Center for Studies in Criminal Justice).

20. H. W. Mattick (1966) *The Unexamined Death* (Chicago: John Howard Association).

21. Mattick, *Unexamined Death.*

22. Zeisel, *Data on Jury Attitudes.*

23. C. H. S. Jayewardene and A. Singh (1976) "Ottawans and the Death Penalty: A Public Opinion Survey" (Unpublished Manuscript. University of Ottawa).

24. Canadian Correctional Chaplains' Association (1970) *Religion and the Death Penalty* (Winnipeg: Canadian Correctional Chaplains' Association).

25. Canadian Correctional Chaplains' Association, *Religion and Death Penalty.*

26. Joint Committee of the Senate and the House of Commons on Capital Punishment, Corporal Punishment and Lotteries (1956) *Report* (Ottawa: Queen's Printer).

27. G. Favreau (1965) *Capital Punishment* (Ottawa: Queen's Printer).

28. *Ottawa Citizen* (1971) November 8th.

29. *Kingston Whig Standard* (1972) March 9th.

30. *Kingston Whig Standard* (1972) March 9th.

31. Favreau, *Capital Punishment.*

32. *Ottawa Citizen* (1973) February 11th.

33. *Canadian Bar Review* (1954) "The Abolition of Capital Punishment." *Canadian Bar Review.* 32, 485-519.

34. P. J. O. Hearn (1956) "Criminal Law – Capital Punishment, Corporal Punishment, Lotteries, Joint Committee Reports." *Canadian Bar Review,* 32, 844-855.

35. E. L. H. Taylor (1958) "A Secular Revolution in Christian Disguise." *Canadian Bar Journal,* 1, 41-46.

36. J. D. Morton (1959) "Murder Most Foul." *Canadian Bar Journal,* 2, 114-120.

37. W. B. Hagarty (1960) "Capital Punishment Should Be Retained." *Canadian Bar Journal,* 3, 42-51.

38. Canada (1961) *Proceedings of the Standing Committee on Banking and Commerce to whom was referred the Bill C-92 entitled: An Act to Amend the Criminal Code (Capital Murder) 27.6.1961* (Ottawa: Queen's Printer).

39. Joint Committee of the Senate and the House of Commons on Capital Punishment, Corporal Punishment and Lotteries (1955) *Minutes of Proceedings and Evidence. Witness: J. Alex Edmison* (Ottawa: Queen's Printer).

40. E. Gowers (1956) *A Life for a Life. The Problem of Capital Punishment* (London: Chatts and Winders).

41. Y. Dandurand and M. E. Fontaine (1972) "Public Opinion and the Death Penalty" (Unpublished manuscript. University of Ottawa).

42. T. Sellin (1959) *The Death Penalty* (Philadelphia: The American Law Institute).

43. M. Rokeach (1960) *The Open and Closed Mind* (New York: Basic Books). M. Rokeach (1969) *Beliefs, Attitudes and Values* (San Francisco: Jorsey-Bass).

44. M. Rokeach, *The Open and Closed Mind.*

45. C. H. S. Jayewardene and A. Singh (1976) *Public Opinion Polls and the Death Penalty.* Paper. American Society of Criminology. November, Tucson.

8

The Alternative of Life Imprisonment

The Canadian data on murder during the period 1965-1970 (Table 8-1) reveal a negative correlation between the incidence of murder and both the expectancy of death as punishment ($r = -0.88$) and the expectancy of life imprisonment ($r = -0.77$). These correlations suggest that these two punishments do exert some deterrent influence. But before this interpretation is accepted as definitive, it must be pointed out that there is a strong positive correlation between the incidence of murder and the expectancy of term imprisonment as punishment for it ($r = 0.98$). This correlation, together with the other two, suggests that there is a threshold value below which punishment is both meaningless and useless. But, as the mandatory punishment for capital murder is death and for noncapital murder is life imprisonment, the imposition of term imprisonment for murder shows that all cases that are designated murder and that are consequently utilized in studies of deterrence are not murder. Included among them are cases of manslaughter for which the threatened punishment is not death. In the interpretation of the correlations, this fact must necessarily be taken into consideration without failing, however, to consider the possibility that the situation may itself be a function of the moratorium on the penalty of death.

The purpose of the penalty of death, the deterrent argument implies, is to prevent the killing of human beings. The argument avers that when the state kills human beings, it prevents the individual from killing. As the penalty of death involves killing, what is pertinent to the deterrent argument is not just the killings that are done by the individual but the killings by the state as well. The relationship between the expectancy of death as punishment and the murder rate in Canada, 1965-1970, is expressed mathematically by the equation $Y = e^{(0.6820 - 0.1728X)}$ where Y is the murder rate and X the expectancy of death as punishment. This equation indicates that during the period when the death penalty was not imposed in Canada, the average annual number of homicides was 244 (assuming a population of 20 million). If the penalty of death was imposed during the period of 1965-1970 as it was during the period 1956-1960, the equation expressing the relationship between the expectancy of death as punishment and the murder rates suggests that there would have been an annual average of 236 killings.

The debate on capital punishment has always proceeded on the assumption that if the penalty is on the statute books, every single homicide offender would suffer an inevitable fate. But nothing is further from the truth. Even

Table 8-1

Relationship of Murder Rates and the Expectancy of Punishment (1965-1970)

Year	Murder Rate	Death	Expectancy of Life Imprisonment	Expectancy of Term Imprisonment
1965	1.5	0.2	16.8	20.0
1966	1.3	0.2	16.2	18.1
1967	1.6	0.1	15.9	19.4
1968	1.8	0.0	17.1	21.7
1969	1.9	0.0	14.1	22.3
1970	2.3	0.0	13.5	24.6

Regression Equations
  Murder Rate and Expectancy of Death
$$Y = e^{(0.6820 - 0.1728X)} \qquad r = -0.88$$

  Murder Rate and Expectancy of Life Imprisonment
$$Y = e^{(0.2117 - 0.1011X)} \qquad r = -0.77$$

  Murder Rate and Expectancy of Term Imprisonment
$$Y = e^{(0.0893X - 1.2290)} \qquad r = 0.98$$

Note: The murder rate is that reported by the police and published in Dominion Bureau of Statistics: *Murder Statistics.*
  The Expectancy of Punishment has been computed from the judicial adjudication of murder cases in the five years preceding.
  Murder rate is per 100,000 population.
  Expectancies of punishment are percentages (chances in a hundred).

when the homicide offender is convicted of murder — the offence which carries the penalty of death — the Royal Prerogative of Mercy remains to prevent the execution. The trend the world over has been fewer and fewer executions.[1] During the period 1956-1960, only 20 percent of those convicted of murder were executed in Canada.[2] The proportion has become even smaller with the passage of time. The analysis of the fate of persons condemned to death during the period 1957-1962, when the penalty of death existed on the statute books, when it was imposed and when it was inflicted, shows that the Royal Prerogative of Mercy was invariably exercised when the offender was under 20 years of age, when there was no apparent motive, or the motive was jealousy, a murder and suicide plan, or a sudden quarrel, and when the death sentence carried a jury and judge recommendation for mercy. In other cases too the Royal Prerogative of Mercy was exercised seemingly on a random basis. With this pattern the random exercise of the Royal Prerogative of Mercy and consequently the execution of the condemned person was only possible in three cases in the years 1963, 1964 and 1965.[3] Under such circumstances, the de jure retention of the death penalty would have resulted in an average annual of more than the 236 killings that could have been expected during the period 1965-1970 if the 1956-1960 conditions prevailed.

Whenever the penalty of death has been abolished, life imprisonment has been prescribed as the substitute punishment. A committee of the United Church of Canada, after due deliberation, concluded that life imprisonment was the appropriate substitute for the penalty of death.[4] Unfortunately, the reasoning behind this conclusion is not made explicit. Legislative debates on the abolition have usually centered on the propriety of the death penalty: rarely has the propriety of the substitute been discussed. The deterrent effect of the penalty of death has always been debated and studied: seldom has the deterrent effect of the substitute been so subjected. Supposedly the next most severe punishment, life imprisonment has always presented itself as a sine qua non for the abolition, suggesting a strong belief on the part of both retentionists and abolitionists in the deterrence of punishment and a deterrence that appears to be influenced by severity. In the Canadian movement against the penalty of death, the propriety of life imprisonment as an alternative for murder has been debated. In this debate,[5] it was contended that life imprisonment was a superior deterrent than death, as first, it removed the offender from society (which death did), second, it removed more offenders from society than death because of the less stringent proof of guilt required for conviction, and third, it was a continuous punishment rather than the monentary punishment that death was. In addition to this, life imprisonment, it was contended, did not carry with it the irrevocability of error that death did, and it offered an opportunity for rehabilitation, which death did not.

The Canadian data showing a negative correlation between the expectancy of life imprisonment as punishment and the incidence of murder suggest that the threat of life imprisonment is a deterrent. The relationship between the two is mathematically expressible in the equation $Y = e^{(0.2117 - 0.1011X)}$ where Y is the murder rate and X the expectancy of life imprisonment as punishment. According to this relationship the Canadian murder rate would be reduced to premoratorium proportions if the expectancy was raised from its present 15 percent to 20 percent. As life imprisonment is the mandatory punishment for murder that was noncapitalized with the moratorium, this expectancy can be increased only if more cases designated murder are adjudicated murder. The premoratorium categorization would give an expectancy of life imprisonment of 20 percent. The reduced expectancy during present times has been produced not by the moratorium on the penalty of death but by the increase in the proportion of cases resulting in convictions of manslaughter and the decrease in the proportion of cases resulting in convictions of murder witnessed in Canada in recent times.

An objection to life imprisonment as punishment for murder lies in the definition of life. It has been contended that murderers sentenced to life imprisonment would be released after they had served a short period of time and thereby not only not suffer their just punishment but also pose a definite threat to society.[6] Although people condemned to life imprisonment do die in prison, no individual has been required to remain in prison until death. Usually persons sentenced to life imprisonment are released after variable periods of time, converting the de jure life imprisonment to a de facto term imprisonment. An analysis of the period of time a lifer spent in prison in England led to the conclusion that in 1866 the minimum was twenty years while in 1900 this was the maximum. In 1939 a lifer was released after he or she had served ten to thirteen years while after the World War II life had come to mean six to ten years.[7] The recent Canadian experience has been an increase rather than a decrease in the number of years a murder convict spends in prison. Capital convicts released during the period 1968 through 1971 spent an average of 13.5 years in prison. This was exclusive of one convict who spent forty years. Capital murderers released in the period 1961-1967 had an average imprisonment of twelve years. Noncapital murderers too spend a longer period in prison now than they did before. For those released after 1968 the average was 7.8 years, for those released before, 6.2 years.[8]

The actual period of time that a lifer is compelled to remain in prison varies from time to time, from place to place, and from individual to individual. Sometimes this period is excessively short, and sometimes it is unduly long. But seldom or never is it the entirety of natural life. The exact moment of release is generally determined by a clinical evaluation of the probability of recidivism, which though frequently correct, surpasses the comprehension of most people, The unpredictability of the period of imprisonment that a lifer must serve has forced some legislatures to fix a minimum period that a person sentenced to penal servitude for life for murder should serve before release, when abolishing the penalty of death.[9] In Canada, the same effect has been achieved through regulations adopted under the Parole Act specifying the minimum period that must be served before parole is granted. In the case of a lifer, serving a commuted death sentence, this period has been fixed at ten years. This action suggests that though rehabilitation and reformation are the verbalized goals of the societal reaction to crime, when the crime is murder, the retributory element stealthily creeps in. In this connection, Barry points out, that in Australia when death sentences are commuted, a high maximum and a substantial minimum term are imposed because of the pressure of public feeling.[10]

The very concern over the definition of life does reflect this underlying orientation. If we assume that there are 500 first offence murders every year and that 15 percent of these remain unsolved and 40 percent end in a conviction of murder, as was the situation in 1970,[11] the probability that an individual would commit a second murder after having committed a first[12] shows that convicted murderers during the period 1970-2000 would add a total of forty five if incarcerated for ten years, thirty one if incarcerated for fifteen years, twenty three if incarcerated for twenty years, and sixteen if incarcerated for twenty five years by the year 2000.[a] Thus, the difference between ten-years and twenty five-years incarceration is an average of an additional murder per year. The murderers who remain undetected in the 15 percent that remain unsolved would, in contradistinction, be responsible for an additional 179 by the year 2000.[b] These calculations take into account only the physical effects of incarceration. A demand for an increase in the period of incarceration of persons sentenced to life imprisonment becomes meaningful only when a psychological component is attributed to the threat of punishment. This psychological component is the increase in the fear to commit that an increase in the severity of the threatened punishment promotes. At the present moment the psychological component is a theoretically assumed supposition: it is not an empirically demonstrated fact. Even if it were, its actualization, as Henshell and Carey point out,[13] is dependent on the public awareness of the connotation of life imprisonment.

Marcel contends that the denial to the state of its right to take the life of a member of the community connotes the restoration to the individual of hope of return to the community some day.[14] In consequence, the substitute penalty should be determined with this objective in view. Also to be considered was the fact that society had to be protected from a repetition of the act. Taking both these factors into consideration he concludes: "All that should be imposed is a period of trial, as specified by the law, for the term ordered by the court, and under the control of prison services," pointing out that the idea has been expressed by many penologists and criminologists.[15] Both these aims would be met, Sheldon Glueck and Eleanor Glueck point out, if the substitute was an indefinite sentence.[16] Macdonald also concurs with this view.[17] If this were the case, the onus of determining the period of incarceration falls on the correctional services, carrying the implications first that the convicted murderer is in need of rehabilitation and second that the staff of the correctional services are competent to effect this rehabilitation. Arguing from the same premise of a dual

---

[a]For these computations those committing murder in any one year were treated as a cohort aged twenty-five years (the average age of a murderer). Using age-specific murder rates (Chapter 2) and assuming that a murderer was forty times as likely to commit a second murder as to commit a first (Chapter 4) the number of murders that the 1970 cohort would commit after release from incarceration for the various time periods, by the year 2000, was computed. From this, the average per cohort year after release was obtained. The total number of cohort years after release for all the cohorts 1970-2000 by year 2000 was determined, and the total number of murders they would commit calculated. It is realized that this method gives only a rough figure. The accurate figure calculated with the use of more mathematically sophisticated techniques is unlikely to give a different figure rounded to the nearest whole number.

[b]The method of calculation adopted here was the same as that adopted in the case of convicted murderers.

function of the substitute but stressing the protection of society rather than the rehabilitation of the offender, Normandeau suggests that the threat of death in the penal code should be substituted with a threat of a maximum term of imprisonment of ten or fifteen years. In addition, the offender should be required to compensate the victim's family with contribution from income from employment.[18] The adoption of Normandeau's suggestion would result in the infliction of a penalty severer than what the criminal is now called on to suffer. The actual period of incarceration may remain substantially the same. The de jure life imprisonment that substituted death has been shown to be a de facto term imprisonment of 7.8 to 13.5 years in Canada. The de facto term imprisonment of a ten to fifteen-year sentence is not likely to be very much less. The compensation element, however, is an added punishment. Though essentially restitutive, it is nonetheless an imposition to the person sentenced to pay.

Notes

1. C. H. Patrick (1965) "The Status of Capital Punishment. A World Perspective." *Jour. Crim. Law Criminol.*, 55, 397-411.

2. G. Favreau (1965) *Capital Punishment* (Ottawa: Queen's Printer).

3. C. H. S. Jayewardene (1972) "The Canadian Movement Against the Death Penalty." *Canad. Jour. Criminol. Correct.*, 14, 366-391.

4. United Church of Canada (1960) *Alternatives to Capital Punishment* (Toronto: United Church of Canada, Board of Evangelism).

5. Canada (1917) *Debates: House of Commons.* 12th Parliament, 7th Session. 325-334, 617-642, 1012-1017.

6. Canada (1917) *Debates: House of Commons.*

7. Patrick, "Status of Capital Punishment," 397-411.

8. *Ottawa Citizen* (1973) February 6th.

9. M. Knight (1964) "The Irish Criminal Justice Act. 1964." *Justice Peace Loc. Govmn. Rev.*, 127, 674-676.

10. J. V. Barry (1968) "Views on the Alternative to Capital Punishment and the Commutation of Sentences," in B. Jones, *The Penalty is Death* (Melbourne: Sun Books).

11. See Chapter 2.

12. See Chapter 4.

13. R. L. Henshel and S. H. Carey (1972) *Deviance, Deterrence and Knowledge of Sanctions.* Paper. Eastern Sociological Meetings (Boston, April).

14. United Nations (1960) *Capital Punishment* (New York: United Nations).

15. United Nations, *Capital Punishment.*

16. S. Glueck and E. Glueck. "Beyond Capital Punishment," in Faculdade de Direito da Universidade ce Coimbra: *Pena de Morte.* Vol. 1, 267-269, quoted in B. Grenier (1972) *Capital Punishment: New Material 1965-1970* (Ottawa: Queen's Printer).

17. J. M. Macdonald (1961) *The Murderer and His Victim* (Springfield, Ill.: C. C. Thomas).

18. A. Normandeau (1964) "La peine de mort au Canada." *Rev. de droit penal criminol.,* 46, 547-559.

9

Five Years After—The Reaction of Parliament

On December 29, 1972, the five-year moratorium on the penalty of death came to an end, and the Canadian law on murder reverted to the premoratorium status. If, as has been contended earlier,[1] the moratorium is viewed as an experiment in which the validity of divergent contentions were to be ascertained, the reversal to the premoratorium status must be taken as a verdict that the experiment was a dismal failure. But this certainly is not the case. The twenty-eighth Parliament had been dissolved: a general election had been held and the twenty-ninth Parliament was being assembled only on January 4th. There were, of course, some members of Parliament who were convinced that the moratorium was the biggest mistake that Canada had ever made. There were others who were equally convinced that the moratorium had proved the abolitionists' contentions. There were still others who felt that the question had not been satisfactorily answered and that an extension of the moratorium was needed for the scientific evaluation of the results. Prior to the dissolution of Parliament, there were indications that a return to the status of the premoratorium period was unlikely: Justice Minister Turner had publicly stated that it was the intention of the government to abolish the penalty of death.[2] But it does not appear that it was the intention of the government to ram down the throats of the people a piece of legislation that had its base in irrational emotion. Solicitor General Goyer was preparing for the new debate with an evaluation of the moratorium. Grenier had been commissioned to update the material in Favreau's *Capital Punishment*,[3] and Fattah had been commissioned to study the deterrent effect of the death penalty with special reference to murder in Canada during the moratorium.[4]

In 1973, Statistics Canada published a special study of murder statistics.[5] Prepared by Stankiewicz-Bleszynski, this study presents statistics relating to murder in Canada as was presented in the annual *Murder Statistics* publication of the Dominion Bureau of Statistics but without limiting itself to the current and few previous years. It deals with murders committed in Canada during the ten year period 1961-1970. These statistics show, as has been pointed out earlier,[6] that the murder rate has increased over the period under study, and the nature of murder, judged in terms of the victim-offender relationship has changed. The study itself is a presentation of statistical data with little or no attempt at interpretation. In this presentation it is pointed out that the number of persons charged with murder are less than the number of persons killed. This difference is attributed to the suicide of some murderers and the murder cases that remain unsolved. In addition to the usual statistical data, the publication presents three special studies. The first—*Murder during the Commission of other Criminal Act 1961-1970*—is an updating of a previous study.[7] It gives the spatial and temporal distribution of these murders during the period 1961-1970, and the types of crimes in the commission of which the murder was committed. Robbery, it should perhaps be pointed out, takes pride of place. The second study entitled *10 Year Firearm Study* deals with murders committed with firearms. Such cases constituted 44.1 percent of all murders. The third is a *10 Year Study of Murder during the Commission of the Criminal Act of Rape or Sexual Assault 1961-1970.* During the period under study there were a total of eighty-nine incidents involving ninety-six victims and sixty-six suspects with 29.2 percent of the cases remaining unsolved.

The figures presented by Statistics Canada, as has been pointed out earlier,[8] do indicate an increase in the incidence of murder. Fattah accepts this position but argues that this increase cannot be attributed to the moratorium on the penalty of death. His contention has its basis in a number of characteristics of murder and crime in Canada, which his analysis has demonstrated. First, there is a relentless increase in murder rates only when Canada is considered as a whole. Murder rates have actually decreased in certain provinces since capital punishment was legally suspended. Second, murder is not the only crime that has shown an increase. There has been an increase in other crimes of violence as well—crimes of violence that did not carry the threat of death; and what is relevant here is the fact that the increase in these crimes of violence was much greater than the increase in the number of murders. Third, the changes that have occurred in the categories of murder for which the death penalty is still threatened, such as the murder of police, do not lend any credence to the contention that the death penalty deters.[9]

The purpose of Grenier's compilation on capital punishment is succinctly stated in his concluding paragraph:

The approach taken to the death penalty is based on moral, philosophical and religious factors; it involves the emotions as much as logical reasoning. Many supporters of either viewpoint are unyielding, and their convictions spring from the depths of their being. It has been said that research and the collection of objective data on capital punishment would not weaken preconceived ideas, and would not contribute to the progress of the debate. The answer to this is that some individuals are still undecided, and the presentation of concrete and objective facts could aid them in coming to their decision. It is true that discussions on the death penalty are suffused with emotion, but it is precisely the desire to get rid of emotionalism and give the debate a more realistic tone, that justifies the presentation of data and figures. This is the objective which the 1965 publication and this paper on capital punishment have sought to achieve.[10]

Describing the changes that have occurred all over the world after 1965 and enumerating the arguments that have been used in debates on the penalty of death, Grenier presents a document with abundant raw data to scientifically test the arguments. The document is objective and uncommitted leaving readers to come to their own conclusions.

On January 11, 1973, Solicitor General Warren Allmand introduced legislation to extend the five-year moratorium on the penalty of death for an additional period of five years. Members of parliament were permitted a free vote, carrying, of course, the connotation that they could vote according to the dictates of their conscience rather than along party lines. Analysis of the voting behaviour of members of parliament in the capital punishment debates of 1966 and 1967 indicate that the term "free vote" carries a slightly different connotation. In 1966, 255 members of parliament voted defeating the bill by a majority of 31. In 1967, 175 voted passing the bill by a majority of 35. If members of parliament are assumed not to have altered their position—and there is no reason why this assumption would be incorrect—it is seen from Table 9-1 that the passage of the 1967 bill was primarily due to more retentionists than abolitionists refraining from voting. The greatest number refraining were members of the Liberal Party. Of these people nearly 70 percent of the retentionists did not voice their opposition to abolition in 1967. The two debates have two characteristics that differentiate them. First the 1966 bill was a private member's one about which the government was not too enthusiastic, while the 1967 bill was a government one that the government wanted to see translated into law. On the basis of this differentiation the reduced opposition to abolition in 1967 could be considered a reflection of government approval. When the government approves a bill, and the vote is free, opposition to the bill by members of the government party remains unexpressed. If the approval is absent, the opposition is expressed. More important, perhaps, is the second characteristic. The 1966 bill called for abolition presumably for all time: the 1967 bill called for suspension for a five-year

Table 9-1
Voting at the 1966 and 1967 Debates on Capital Punishment

Party	1966		1967	
	For	Against	For	Against
Liberal	73	51	72	15
Conservative	17	79	16	47
N.D.P.	21	0	17	0
Creditiste	0	9	0	6
Social Credit	1	4	0	2
Total	112	143	105	70

Source: Y. Dandurand and M. E. Fontaine (1972) "Public Opinion and the Death Penalty" (Unpublished Manuscript. University of Ottawa). Reprinted with permission.

period. This difference could perhaps have removed much of the objection
tempting retentionists to abstain from voting.[11]

An additional factor exists to complicate the 1973 debate. The government
is a minority government dependent for its existence on the good will of the
opposition parties. Early in its life, there was no way in knowing how long this
existence would be. With a general election possible at any moment, members
of Parliament had to decide whether their consciences, by which they were to
be guided in voting, were influenced by only the moral and utilitarian propriety
of the penalty or by public opinion as well. There were some members, like
Peter Reilly, who felt that the death penalty served no useful purpose and
declared their intention to vote for the bill.[12] There were others, like Tom
Cossitt, who felt the same way but thought they were obliged to bow to public
opinion.[13] There were still others like John Diefenbaker—an abolitionist—who
believed that members of Parliament were not delegates bound to act on instructions from their ridings, presumed to have minds of their own, and elected
to deal conscientiously with public affairs, but who, nonetheless, would have
the question on capital punishment referred to some other body such as the
Supreme Court.[14] In this connection it is interesting to note that only 91 of
264 MPs responded to a questionnaire on capital punishment sent them by the
Canadian Press, and of them only 72 gave a definite answer. These answers
showed that thirteen Liberal MPs, five Conservative and sixteen N.D.P. MPs
would vote for the bill, while three Liberal MPs, twenty-five Conservative, one
N.D.P., and two Social Credit MPs would vote against. The basis of their decision is unknown. The answers of two Liberal MPs, four Conservatives, and
one N.D.P. MP were not amenable to this analysis.[15]

When the debate began, Nielsen—member for Yukon—argued that Parliament was wasting its time considering the question of capital punishment when
more important problems such as inflation and getting the economy going
again remained unresolved.[16] A similar contention was made by Eldon Wool-
liams, member for Calgary North, who went even further to contend that the
debate on capital punishment was a deliberate attempt by the government to
sweep "under the carpet serious problems of unemployment and inflation and
the suffering and frustration of our senior citizens and those on fixed incomes,
who are waiting for relief."[17] Mr. Nielsen suggested that the debate should be
terminated and the question referred to the Commons justice committee who
could, after due consideration, recommend total abolition, an extension of the
partial ban, the appointment of a Royal Commission to study the subject, or a
national referendum.[18] This suggestion was not prompted, as it appears to be,
by a desire to rest the decision on objective and emotion-free considerations
but by a desire to prevent the further suspension of the penalty. Until new
legislation was passed the country was bound by the premoratorium law.
Opposed to the bill in its existing form was Marcel Prud'homme, Member for

Montreal-St. Denis, who would, however, have voted for it. His opposition stemmed from the belief that the bill did not go far enough. He proposed an amendment that would ban all hanging and require a mandatory twenty-five-year stay in prison.[19]

The arguments used on both sides during the debate were the usual hackneyed ones. It was a deterrent: it was not a deterrent. It was morally right: it was morally wrong. It protected society: it did not protect society. It permitted rehabilitation: it did not permit rehabilitation. It was archaic and barbaric: it was not so. In a debate on a subject like capital punishment when all that could perhaps be said has been said ad nauseam, the usual and hackneyed arguments must necessarily be used. Refreshing, however, was the fact that these arguments, both for and against, were, rightly or wrongly, supported by reference to new facts. The members of Parliament indicated, in their speeches, that they had studied the subject anew considering all available factual material, even though the consideration may have been only a search for available facts that supported their original opinion. The speeches on the bill showed nine Liberal MPs, six Conservatives and six N.D.P. MPs supporting it and four Liberal MPs, seven Conservatives, and three Socreds opposing.[20] With this as the situation, Solicitor General Allmand estimated that the bill would draw enough votes to pass second reading but might not survive third reading in the form it existed. He expressed his willingness to amend the bill and instructed his staff to listen to the debate and note any serious suggestions.[21] His main concern over the possible nonpassage of the bill was not a committment to abolition—though he himself is an acknowledged abolitionist. It was the flood of commutation applications that would follow and the quantity and quality of the work that this would entail.[22] The debate, however, was interrupted on February 1, 1973, for discussion of a resolution on Vietnam and the Export Development Act.

The debate was resumed on May 14, 1973. In the meantime, however, Statistics Canada had released the Crime Statistics for 1971. The murder rate for that year was 2.0 indicating not an increase over the previous year but a decrease. In addition the prospect of an impending election had become an unlikely theoretical possibility. A third factor that could influence the outcome of the debate was a spate of jail breaks at the crucial moment. A large number of prisoners escaped not only from the minimum security institution at Cowansville but also from the maximum security one at St. Vincent de Paul. When the debate resumed Prime Minister Trudeau, Opposition Leader Robert Stanfield, and the leader of the New Democratic Party David Lewis all spoke in support of the bill. Leader of the Social Credit Party Réal Caouette had voiced his opposition in no uncertain terms. The debate concluded on May 29th with the bill being accepted, 139 voting for and 114 voting against. Most members of the Liberal Party voted for the bill, while most members of the

Conservative Party voted against it. The Social Credit Party voted en bloc against the bill while the New Democratic Party members, with the exception of one man, all voted for the bill.

Notes

   1. See Chapter 2.

   2. *Le Devoir* (1971) November 20th.

   3. B. Grenier (1972) *Capital Punishment: New Material 1965-1970* (Ottawa: Queen's Printer).

   4. E. A. Fattah (1972) *A Study of the Deterrent Effect of Capital Punishment with Special Reference to the Canadian Situation* (Ottawa: Queen's Printer).

   5. Statistics Canada (1973) *Murder Statistics. 1961-1970* (Ottawa: Queen's Printer).

   6. See Chapter 4.

   7. Dominion Bureau of Statistics (1971) *Murder Statistics 1970* (Ottawa: Queen's Printer).

   8. See Chapter 4.

   9. Fattah, *Study of Deterrent Effect of Capital Punishment.*

   10. Grenier, *Capital Punishment: New Material.*

   11. See Chapter 1.

   12. *Ottawa Journal* (1973) January 20th.

   13. *Ottawa Journal* (1973) January 20th.

   14. *Ottawa Citizen* (1973) February 10th.

   15. *Ottawa Journal* (1973) February 17th.

   16. *Ottawa Journal* (1973) January 27th.

   17. *Ottawa Journal* (1973) January 30th.

   18. *Ottawa Journal* (1973) January 27th.

   19. *Ottawa Journal* (1973) January 27th.

   20. *The Gazette* (1973) February 1st.

   21. *Ottawa Journal* (1973) February 3rd.

   22. *Ottawa Journal* (1973) February 3rd.

10 Previous Attempts at Abolition

The nonimposition of the penalty of death that followed the 1967 moratorium was not the first occasion on which the use of the penalty was in abeyance in Canada, nor was the movement that resulted in the moratorium the first movement of its kind. A most vigorous movement for the abolition of capital punishment could be said to have taken place during the years 1914-1925. The newspapers during this period are replete with news items, features, articles, letters to the editor, and editorials that dealt with the subject. Spearheading the movement was Robert Bickerdike, financier and underwriter of Montreal. Born on August 17, 1843, in Kingston, Ontario, he was first elected to the Quebec Legislature in 1897. He represented the people of the riding of St. Lawrence-Montreal in the Canadian Parliament during the period 1904-1917.[1] Actually the movement could be considered the crusade of Mr. Bickerdike, though a few others do lay a claim to the role of principal actors. The speeches that Mr. Bickerdike made, the letters he wrote, and the material that he collected[2] all indicate that his obsessional belief in the impropriety of the penalty of death stemmed from the view that "capital punishment was essentially murder, a blot on Christianity, a blight on religion, and a reproach to any nation which allows it to remain on its statute books." This was his invariable argument. It was his main argument, but it was not his sole argument. Whenever it appeared expedient, Mr. Bickerdike did not fail to draw attention to the brutality associated with the execution of the penalty, its inefficacy as a deterrent, the possibility of error, and the waste of human resource that it entails.

The first public manifestation of Mr. Bickerdike's interest in capital punishment came in the form of a private member's bill introduced in Parliament on February 5, 1914.[3] That the government of the day did not take the bill seriously is obvious. After Mr. Bickerdike had finished his introductory speech, a long and impassioned plea interspersed with logical arguments, the Minister of Trade and Commerce, Mr. George E. Foster, congratulated the mover of the bill on the manner in which he had presented it and moved the adjournment of the debate as the subject was too serious a one to be discussed without intensive and extensive study. The government strategy, however, was not to prove successful so easily. The desire of the members, vociferously voiced by F. B. Cawd, member for Carleton, New Brunswick, saw the continuance of the debate although only to meet its inevitable end with the motion for adjournment later on by the then Minister of Justice, Honourable C. J. Doherty. The debate itself, though unsuccessful, made important revelations. It showed that the question, though not a burning one, was not one that did not have any support nor was it one that did not have intense opposition. It was one on which strong views were held, though these views had seldom or never been voiced.

A second attempt to have the penalty of death abolished in Canada was made in 1915 by Robert Bickerdike.[4] On February 12, 1915, Mr. Bickerdike moved the second reading of Bill No. 18 "to amend the Criminal Code and abolish the penalty of death." Because of the absence of the Minister of Justice from Parliament that day, the debate was adjourned and resumed on February 18, 1915, when Justice Minister Doherty attempted to have the debate adjourned, sine die, with the contention that the question was so serious a one that it should only be discussed after members had given it serious consideration. The government strategy failed. The debate was continued, and the question was put to the House only to be negated. Undaunted, Mr. Bickerdike made a third attempt to have capital punishment abolished in 1916. This time too the 1915 drama was repeated. There was the government attempt to have the bill withdrawn in its early stages. This attempt, however, was made by Prime Minister Sir Robert Borden, and it was more determined. There was the continuation of the debate. There was the final division and the defeat of the motion.[5]

Mr. Bickerdike's last and final effort to have the penalty abolished was made on January 31, 1917, when he moved the second reading of Bill No. 3 "to amend the Criminal Code and to abolish the penalty of death." The bill was debated on April 19th and May 2nd when it was put to the vote and defeated.[6] Associated with this bill were two other motions, both moved by Mr. Bickerdike. The first called for the abolition of capital punishment for women and children but was ruled out of order by the Speaker as it was closely akin to the bill that had been discussed.[7] The second was designed to save from execution an eighteen-year-old youth who had been sentenced to death. This motion too was ruled out of order by the Speaker on Justice, Minister Doherty pointing out that it dealt with the question of clemency, which was a Royal Prerogative and hence a matter that was not subject to debate in the House of Commons.

Mr. Bickerdike's efforts at abolition in Parliament were not limited to the sponsorship of bills for the abolition. Whenever the opportunity arose in the House of Commons, Mr. Bickerdike never failed to make a plea for the abolition. Thus when prison reforms were being discussed both in 1914[8] and in 1915[9] Mr. Bickerdike made pointed remarks on the inadvisability of having capital punishment on the country's statute books. He also conducted considerable propaganda in different parts of the country, speaking on the subject and writing articles and letters to the newspapers.

If he could not secure the de jure abolition of the penalty, Mr. Bickerdike attempted to have it abolished de facto by pleading for, and obtaining, the reprieve of condemned prisoners. This, he did through penal reform associations he helped to found. The first such association was the Criminal Reform Association.

Founded in 1915, this association had as its main aim prison reform, but Mr. Bickerdike pushed the advocacy of the abolition of capital punishment to such an extent, much to the chagrin of his colleagues, that he was forced to split away and form another association—the National Criminal Reform Association. In 1919, this association merged with the Honour League, founded in 1916 to give assistance to those discharged from prisons and penitentiaries, under the name of the Canadian Prisoners' Welfare Association and the presidency of Mr. Bickerdike. Attempts to utilize it in the campaign against capital punishment threatened a split that was averted by the extension of its ostensible purpose—"to promote by all lawful means the welfare of prisoners"—to include condemned prisoners. This extension permitted the Association to be against execution in each and every case where sentence was pronounced, without being against the penalty of death in its abstract form. Thus, the Association, while not campaigning against the penalty of death, sought to secure a reprieve for condemned prisoners whenever such condemnations occurred.

The annual reports of this Association contain claims of success in this activity. The Association did move to obtain a reprieve in a number of cases and succeeded in many, but whether the commutation was the result of their moves must remain a matter of speculation. The statistical information on executions presented in the Report of the Joint Committee of the Senate and House of Commons on Capital Punishment[10] does not indicate any change in commutation policy. This Association was most active in this respect in the eleven year period 1915-1925. During this period 118 of 254 sentenced to death were executed. During the eleven-year period immediately prior (1904-1914) 81 of the 173 condemned were executed and in the eleven-year period immediately after, 1926-1936, 140 of the 233 condemned. Though the proportion executed was least during the period 1915-1925 (46.5 percent) the proportions executed during the period before (46.8 percent) and during the period after (60.1 percent) are not sufficiently different statistically to indicate the influence of some extraneous force.

In the closing years of Mr. Bickerdike's life, Canada was not much nearer abolition than when he introduced his first bill in 1914. Mr. Bickerdike had not presented himself as a candidate for the thirteenth Parliament, and in that Parliament there were no bills introduced to abolish the penalty. There appears to have been a lull in the movement, though not without the newspapers periodically referring to some aspect of the subject. Thus newspapers carried in December 1921 the information that the last sentence of death in the Montreal district was pronounced on three men who had killed a farmer in St. Solpice in the winter of 1919 and that thereafter Grace Moreno had been sentenced to life imprisonment for killing a man.[11] They also pointed out that murder in Canada was most frequently committed with small firearms and that the control of this crime called for not the abolition of the penalty of death but legislation restricting the possession of such weapons.[12] The interest that was maintained on the subject was sporadically converted into enthusiastic outbursts by some special characteristic of a case such as the hanging of Thomas Fletcher in Winnipeg in 1918, when a miscalculation on the part of the hangman forced the unfortunate to strangle for forty-four minutes before he died, and the birth of twins in 1920 to Marie Anne Houde (Mme Gagnon) of Quebec while under the sentence of death.

The movement for abolition had, by 1924, gained sufficient momentum to see another legislative bid at abolition. The public opinion at this time did not appear to be any different from that when Mr. Bickerdike introduced his bills. The Trades and Labour Council had declared itself in favour of abolition,[13] newspapers had carried editorials expressing their inability to endorse such a move,[14] and the Committee on Criminology of the Social Service Council of Canada presented a report that concluded with the statement that: "its members did not, while still open to conviction, feel warranted to recommending at present the abolition of capital punishment."[15]

Yet a bill was introduced in Parliament by Reverend William Irvine, member for Calgary East, to abolish the penalty of death. The bill was debated on April 11, 1924, with Justice Minister Ernest Lapointe and Solicitor General E. J. McMurray opposing it and Railways Minister G. P. Graham supporting it. A free vote resulted in its defeat—twenty-nine for and ninety-two against.[16] The anti-capital punishment sentiment in the country reached its peak only after the bill had been debated. It stemmed from the sensibilities of the community being touched by the condemnation to death of four youths for the murder, during robbery, of an old man. It provoked the Canadian Bar Association to observe that

while the wide-spread compassion for the doomed men redounded to the credit of the Candadian people, the fate of the malefactors should not provide any more encouragement for another possible bid at abolition than the previous bid had received.[17]

Seventeenth-century Canadian Society has been likened to any other society of that time with punishments that were severe and cruel.[18] As the law that was in force in Canada during this period was the French law, considered harsh as were all laws of that period, the situation in Canada had been assumed to have been no different from that in France. Yet, though public hangings, mutilations, and disembowelment were the punishments prescribed and pronounced, they were not the ones inflicted.[19] The discrepancy between the pronounced and the inflicted punishments had been attributed by Lomer[20] to the difficulty of finding a hangman, but Boyer[21] attributes it to a modification of the law. According to him the customs of the native populations of Canada influenced considerably the colonizing French, forcing them to adopt an orientation entirely different to that obtained in their homeland. Death, to both the Indians[22] and the Eskimoes[23] was to be inflicted not in a spirit of vengeance, but as a last resort to safeguard the community as a whole. Thus it was the punishment for witchcraft or for treason. It was even the punishment for laziness that jeopardized the winter food supply of the group. It was the punishment for murder only when it was thought that the spirit of the murdered man was calling for appeasement, threatening destruction to all. The French too apparently adopted the same attitude. Murder meant the death of one man: there was no need to make it mean the death of two. The smallness of the population and the vastness of the country had made the natives of Canada consider capital punishment a senseless depletion of their meager human resources. Perhaps this logic was forcibly driven home to the French trying to gain and maintain control of a land where everything seemed against them.[24] Perhaps the smallness of the population made them a closely knit group in which the imposition of drastic penalties was not considered necessary to induce conformity.[25]

After the conquest of Canada, its formal cession and the establishment of the Province of Quebec in 1763, the prevailing system of justice was replaced with the laws of England by the Royal Proclamation of 1763.[26] The laws of England were no different from the laws of France. The punishments prescribed were equally severe and equally cruel, with no less than 120 crimes for which the death penalty was prescribed.[27] What the Royal Proclamation apparently did was to change a strictly de jure situation into a de facto one with the public executions that the law demanded serving as a form of entertainment and amusement.[28] Even then, there seems to have been a selective enforcement. Some sentenced to death were executed, while others got off with no more than a year in jail,[29] with the latter category increasing in numbers till by 1830, we were told, the sentence of death was almost a meaningless pronouncement.[30]

The number of capital crimes were reduced in 1859. In the Consolidated Statutes of Canada, the penalty of death was provided for murder, treason, rape, administering poison, wounding with intent to commit murder, unlawfully abusing a girl under ten, buggery with man or beast, robbery with wounding, burglary with assault, arson, setting fire, casting away a ship, and exhibiting a false signal endangering a ship.[31] Further changes were to follow. In 1865 the death penalty was abolished in all cases except murder, treason, and rape. Since then it was mandatory only in the case of murder, and it has never been imposed or inflicted for rape.[32] In 1869, public executions were abolished with Patrick James Whelan, the assassin of Thomas D'Arcy McGee, being the last man to be publicly executed in Canada. He was hanged in the Carleton County Jail in Ottawa on February 11, 1869, in the presence of a large crowd that had braved the zero temperature of that February morning and had to be kept in order by a large force of city police.[33]

Of special significance for the penalty of death was the rebellion of 1837. Robert Nelson, the cranky surgeon brother of the burly English doctor, Wolfred Nelson, who had led the patriots of Richelieu, found crowds of patriots in the

border villages, leaderless. Louis Joseph Papineau, on whom were pinned the
hopes of the harassed and frustrated Canadians, disease and political tension
bedevilled, had failed to obtain the much needed help he had hoped to get from
the United States. Surrounded by equally frustrated advisors on the verge of
what would be called mutiny, Papineau had virtually abandoned the rebels
and the rebellion. Nelson marched the rebels across the border into Canada on
February 28, 1838, and, having done so, read a Declaration declaring the Re-
public of Canada signed by him as its first President.[34] In this Declaration, he
abolished the penalty of death.[35]

The abolition was really meaningless for Nelson had no power to do so, but
it was given content and meaning by the English administrators who having
quelled the rebellion were seeking to establish an enduring peace. The rebellion
had seen the slaughter of many men—the victims of a senseless war. Many more
had been claimed by the penalty of death—the then just penalty for treason.[36]
Earl Durham, who had been sent to Canada entrusted with the task of restoring
law and order, however wanted to do so not in a spirit of revenge but in one of
justice with mercy. Aided by an inability to empanel juries who were willing
to try the rebels fairly, Durham took the law into his own hands, exiling leaders
and releasing the followers.[37] The penalty of death, the prescribed penalty for
treason, was not imposed or inflicted on them. This noninfliction marked the
beginning of a twenty-year period during which the penalty was de facto, though
not de jure abolished.[38] It was only in 1859, when the macabre spectacle of the
wanton destruction that was the rebellion of 1837 was being relegated into the
realm of the old wives' tales, that the death penalty again began to be inflicted.
In this connection it is perhaps interesting to note that total abolition was once
legislatively acclaimed in the Assembly at Quebec, though to be thrown out
in the Senate by the casting vote of the Speaker alone.[39]

What effect this abolition had cannot at this time be assessed. However,
had it not been for the Royal Prerogative of Mercy, Whelan would have no place
in the pages of Canadian History as the last to be publicly executed. Thomas
D'Arcy McGee, for whose murder Whelan suffered death, had been tried, convicted, and sentenced to death, with eight others, for the part they played in
the Young Ireland disorders of 1848. Queen Victoria had commuted their
sentences and had them transported to the penal colonies of Australia. In
1871, when Sir Charles Duffy was elected Prime Minister of Australia, the
Queen had been informed that he was one whose life she had saved twenty-
three years earlier. Curious, she had the later lives of the remaining eight
traced only to find that one of them, Thomas Meager, was Governor of Montana,
another Richard O'Gorman was Governor-General of New Foundland, two
others Terrence McManus and Patrick Donahue were Brigadier Generals in the
United States Army, one Michael Ireland was Attorney General of Australia, a
post which another of them, Morris Lyene, had held. One John Mitchell was a
prominent politician in New York, while the eighth, Thomas McGee was

President of the Council for the Dominion of Canada. They were all prominent and loyal servants of Her Majesty the Queen and this in spite of their declaration before the pronouncement of sentence: "My Lord, this is our first offence, but not our last. If you will be easy with us this once, we promise on our word as gentlemen to do better next time. And the next time, sure we won't be fools enough to be caught."[40]

Notes

1. *Detroit News Tribune* (1917) February 18th.

2. *The Bickerdike Scrap Book* now in the possession of Professor J. Alex Edmison, Q.C.

3. Canada (1914) *Debates: House of Commons.* 12th Parliament, 3rd Session. 428-511.

4. Canada (1915) *Debates: House of Commons.* 12th Parliament, 5th Session. 127-141, 264-284.

5. Canada (1916) *Debates: House of Commons.* 12th Parliament, 6th Session. 1957-1968.

6. Canada (1917) *Debates: House of Commons.* 12th Parliament, 7th Session. 325-334, 617-642, 1012-1017.

7. Canada (1917) *Debates: House of Commons.* 1017.

8. Canada (1914) *Debates: House of Commons.* 4516-4517.

9. Canada (1915) *Debates: House of Commons.* 1761-1765.

10. Joint Committee of the Senate and the House of Commons on Capital Punishment, Corporal Punishment and Lotteries (1956) *Report* (Ottawa: Queen's Printer).

11. *The Gazette* (1921) December 27th.

12. *The Gazette* (1920) October 4th.

13. *The Gazette* (1923) March 2nd.

14. *Quebec Chronicle* (1923) March 7th.

15. *The Gazette* (1922) February 24th.

16. Canada (1924) *Debates: House of Commons.* 14th Parliament, 3rd Session. 1265-1313.

17. Canadian Bar Review (1924) Crime and its Punishment. *Canadian Bar Review,* 2, 569-572.

18. A. R. M. Lomer (1958) *Canadians in the Making* (Toronto: Longmans, Green and Co.).

19. Lomer, *Canadians in the Making.*

20. Lomer, *Canadians in the Making.*

ELETE

21. R. Boyer (1966) *Les Crimes et Les Châtiments au Canada Français du XVII au XX Siècle* (Montreal: Le Cercle du Livre de France).

22. W. B. Newell (1965) *Crime and Justice among the Iroquois Indians* (Montreal: Caughanawaga Historical Society).

23. N. H. H. Graburn (1969) *Eskimos without Igloos* (Boston: Little, Brown & Co.).

24. Boyer, *Les Crimes et Les Châtiments.*

25. Lomer, *Canadians in the Making;* E. Salme (1910) *La Colonisation de la Nouvelle France,* quoted in Boyer, *Les Crimes et Les Châtiments.*

26. W. R. Riddell (1925) "Criminal Courts and Law in Early (Upper) Canada." *Ontario Historical Society's Papers and Records,* 22, 3-14.

27. L. B. Duff (1949) *The County Kerchief* (Toronto: The Ryerson Press).

28. Duff, *County Kerchief.*

29. Dr. Porthwick (n.d.) *History of the Montreal Prison 1784-1886,* quoted in J. Kidman (1947) *The Canadian Prison* (Toronto: The Ryerson Press).

30. Porthwick, *History Montreal Prison.*

31. J. A. Jones (1924) *Pioneer Crimes and Punishments* (Toronto: George N. Morang).

32. W. T. McGrath (1956) *Should Canada Abolish the Gallows and the Lash?* (Winnipeg: Stovel Advocate Press).

33. Duff, *County Kerchief.*

34. J. Schull (1971) *Rebellion* (Toronto: Macmillan of Canada).

35. Boyer, *Les Crimes et Les Châtiments.*

36. Duff, *County Kerchief.*

37. Schull, *Rebellion.*

38. Boyer, *Les Crimes et Les Châtiments.*

39. H. Moh (1873) *Shall Capital Punishment be Abolished?* (Montreal: Daniel Rose).

40. Duff, *County Kerchief.*

Bibliography

Akman, D. D.

1966   Homicides and Assaults in Canadian Penitentiaries. *Canad. Jour. Correct.*, 8: 284-299.

1967   Homicides and Assaults in Canadian Penitentiaries. *Howard Jour. Penol.*, 102-112.

1967   Homicides and Assaults in Canadian Penitentiaries. In T. Sellin: *Capital Punishment* (New York: Harper & Bros.) 161-168.

Andenaes, J.

1952   General Prevention: Illusion or Reality. *Jour. Crim. Law Criminol.*, 43: 176-198.

1966   The General Preventive Effects of Punishment. *Univ. Penn. Law Rev.*, 114: 949.

Anttila, I., Tornud, P., and Westling, A.

1964   Elinkautinen Kuritushuonevangais Rus. *Kriminologen Tutkimuslaitos*, 1: 1-23.

Anttila, I., and Westling, A.

1965   The Pardoning of a Recidivism among Criminals Sentenced to Life Imprisonment. *Scand. Stud. Criminol.*, 1: 13-34.

Bandura, A.

1965   Influence of Model's Reinforcement Contingencies on the Acquisition of Imitative Responses. *Jour. Personality Soc. Psych.*, 1: 589-595.

Barry, J. V.

1968   Views on the Alternative to Capital Punishment and the Commutation of Sentences. In B. Jones: *The Penalty is Death* (Melbourne: Sun Books).

Barzun, J.

1962   In Favour of Capital Punishment. *Amer. Schol.*, 31: 181-191.

1969   In Favour of Capital Punishment. *Crime Delinq.*, 15: 21-28.

Beccaria, C.

1809   *Essay on Crimes and Punishment* (New York: Harper & Row).

Boydell, C. L., and Grindstaff, C. F.

1972   Public Attitude and Legal Sanctions. In C. L. Boydell, C. F. Grindstaff, and P. C. Whitehead: *Deviant Behaviour and Societal Reaction* (Toronto: Holt, Rinehart and Winston).

Boyer, R.

1966   *Les Crimes et Les Châtiments au Canada Français du XVII au XX Siècle* (Montréal: Le Cercle du Livre de France).

Bristow, A. C.
    1963   Police Officer Shootings. A Tactical Evaluation. *Jour. Crim. Law Criminol.*, 54, 93-95
Calgary Herald
    1967   April 22nd.
Campion, D.
    1955   The State Police and the Death Penalty. In Joint Committee of the Senate and the House of Commons on Capital and Corporal Punishment and Lotteries: *Minutes of Proceedings and Evidence: Appendix F* (Ottawa: Queen's Printer).
    1956   The State Police and the Death Penalty. *Congressional Record*, March 6, A 2076-2080.
    1964   Does the Death Penalty Protect State Police? In H. A. Bedeau: *The Death Penalty in America* (Garden City, N. Y.: Anchor Doubleday).
Canada
    1914   *Debates: House of Commons.* 12th Parliament, 3rd Session, 428-511, 4516-4517.
    1915   *Debates: House of Commons.* 12th Parliament, 5th Session, 127-141, 264-284, 1761-1765.
    1916   *Debates: House of Commons.* 12th Parliament, 6th Session, 1957-1968.
    1917   *Debates: House of Commons.* 12th Parliament, 7th Session, 325-334, 617-642, 1012-1017, 1018-1023.
    1924   *Debates: House of Commons.* 14th Parliament, 3rd Session, 1265-1313.
    1948   *Debates: House of Commons.* 20th Parliament, 4th Session, 5148-5188.
    1950   *Debates: House of Commons.* 21st Parliament, 2nd Session, 37, 250, 2088, 3277-3283, 3890.
    1953   *Debates: House of Commons.* 21st Parliament, 7th Session, 2259-2267, 4044-4049.
    1953   *Debates: House of Commons.* 22nd Parliament, 1st Session, 939-958, 1023-1036, 1047-1061.
    1954   *Debates: House of Commons.* 22nd Parliament, 1st Session, 2652.
    1956   *Debates: House of Commons.* 22nd Parliament, 3rd Session, 7491.
    1957   *Debates: House of Commons.* 23rd Parliament, 2496-2576.
    1958   *Debates: House of Commons.* 24th Parliament, 2nd Session, 711-718, 2977-2983.
    1959   *Debates: House of Commons.* 24th Parliament, 2nd Session, 141-143, 2198-2204, 4960-2965.
    1960   *Debates: House of Commons.* 24th Parliament, 3rd Session, 2-3, 39, 492-493, 1186-1187, 1187-1223, 1435-1436, 1441-1474, 1646-1647, 1879, 1885, 2012-2021, 2252, 2252-2253, 4767, 4877-4879, 6410, 7192-7193, 7324-7325, 7529-7533.

1961   *Debates: House of Commons.* 24th Parliament, 4th Session, 3829,
       5220-5248, 5299-5326, 5506-5565, 5879-5915.
1961   *Proceedings of the Standing Committee on Banking and Commerce
       to whom was referred the Bill C-92 entitled: An Act to Amend the
       Criminal Code (Capital Murder) 27.6.1961* (Ottawa: Queen's
       Printer).
1962   *Debates: House of Commons.* 25th Parliament, lst Session, 375,
       2487, 2812.
1963   *Debates: House of Commons.* 25th Parliament, 1st Session, 3382,
       3386-3387.
1963   *Debates: House of Commons.* 26th Parliament, 1st Session, 375.
1964   *Debates: House of Commons.* 26th Parliament, 2nd Session, 1418-
       1426, 4930, 5205.
1965   *Debates: House of Commons.* 26th Parliament, 2nd Session,
       11469, 11628, 12878.
1965   *Debates: House of Commons.* 26th Parliament, 3rd Session, 1-3,
       4-10, 19-58, 64-89, 101-160, 172-207, 217-289, 309-335, 338-
       383, 982, 1150-1151, 1450-1451, 2322, 2417, 2495, 3063-3064.
1966   *Debates: House of Commons.* 27th Parliament, 1st Session, 3067-
       3085, 3095-3158, 3262-3324, 3789-3852, 3865-3911, 5158-5159,
       6752, 8193, 8518, 8605, 10587, 12261, 12397, 12508-12510.
1967   *Debates: House of Commons.* 27th Parliament, 1st Session,
       14706-14707, 15232.
1967   *Debates: House of Commons.* 27th Parliament, 2nd Session, 4977,
       4098, 4103-4118, 4142-4164, 4244-4266, 4274-4293, 4311-4320,
       4336-4357, 4365-4381, 4570-4585, 4604-4621, 4629-4644, 4846-
       4861, 4879-4893.

Canadian Bar Review
1924   "Crime and Its Punishment" *Canad. Bar Rev.* 2: 569-572
1954   "The Abolition of Capital Punishment" *Canad. Bar Rev.* 32: 485-
       519.
Canadian Correctional Chaplains Association
1970   *Religion and the Death Penalty* (Winnipeg: Canadian Correctional
       Chaplains Association).
Cardarelli, A. P.
1968   An Analysis of Police Killed by Criminal Action 1961-1963. *Jour.
       Crim. Law Criminol.,* 59: 447-453.
Chambliss, W. J.
1966   The Deterrent Influence of Punishment. *Crime Delinq.,* 12: 70-75.
Chiricos, T. G., and Waldo, G. P.
1970   Punishment and Crime: An Examination of Some Empirical Evidence.
       Soc. Prob., 18: 200-217.
Claster, D.
1967   Comparison of Risk Perception between Delinquents and

Nondelinquents. *Jour. Crim. Law Criminol.,* 58, 80.
Clinard, M. B.
  1957   *The Sociology of Deviant Behaviour* (New York: Rinehart and Co.).
Creamer, S. J. and Robin, G.
  1970   Assaults on Police. In S. Chapman: *Police Patrol Reader* (Spring-
         field, Ill.: C. C. Thomas) 485-494.
Dandurand, Y., and Fontaine, M. E.
  1972   Public Opinion and the Death Penalty (Unpublished Manuscript.
         University of Ottawa).
Dann, R. H.
  1935   The Deterrent Effect of Capital Punishment. *Friends Social Service
         Series Bull.,* 39.
Detroit News Tribune
  1917   February 18th.
Duff, L. B.
  1949   *The County Kerchief* (Toronto: The Ryerson Press).
Dominion Bureau of Statistics
  1964   *Police Administration Statistics 1963* (Ottawa: Queen's Printer).
  1965   *Police Administration Statistics 1964* (Ottawa: Queen's Printer).
  1966   *Police Administration Statistics 1965* (Ottawa: Queen's Printer).
  1967   *Murder Statistics 1961-1965* (Ottawa: Queen's Printer).
  1967   *Murder Statistics 1966* (Ottawa: Queen's Printer).
  1967   *Police Administration Statistics 1966* (Ottawa: Queen's Printer).
  1968   *Murder Statistics 1967* (Ottawa: Queen's Printer).
  1968   *Police Administration Statistics 1967* (Ottawa: Queen's Printer).
  1969   *Murder Statistics 1968* (Ottawa: Queen's Printer).
  1969   *Police Administration Statistics 1968* (Ottawa: Queen's Printer).
  1970   *Murder Statistics 1969* (Ottawa: Queen's Printer).
  1970   *Police Administration Statistics 1969* (Ottawa: Queen's Printer).
  1971   *Murder Statistics 1970* (Ottawa: Queen's Printer).
  1971   *Police Administration Statistics 1970* (Ottawa: Queen's Printer).
Edmonton Journal
  1972   January 29th.
Fattah, E. A.
  1972   *A Study of the Deterrent Effect of Capital Punishment with Special
         Reference to the Canadian Situation* (Ottawa: Queen's Printer).
Favreau, G.
  1965   *Capital Punishment* (Ottawa: Queen's Printer).
Financial Post
  1946   October 21st.
Giardini, G. I., and Farrow, R. G.
  1952   The Paroling of Capital Offenders. *Ann. Amer. Acad. Pol. Soc. Sci.,*
         284: 85-94.

Gibbs, J. P.
    1968   Crime, Punishment and Deterrence. *Southwestern Soc. Sci. Quart.,*
            48: 515-530.
Globe and Mail
    1948   April 27th.
    1971   April 21st, April 24th, April 29th.
Goetz, R. S.
    1961   Should Ohio Abolish Capital Punishment. *Cleveland Marshall Law
            Rev.,* 10: 365-377.
Goode, W.
    1966   Violence among Inmates. In D. J. Mulvihill, M. M. Tumin, and
            L. A. Curtis: *Crimes of Violence* (Washington, D. C.: Government
            Printing Office) 941-977.
Gowers, E.
    1956   *A Life for a Life. The Problem of Capital Punishment* (London:
            Chatto and Windus).
Graburn, N. H. H.
    1969   *Eskimos without Igloos* (Boston: Little, Brown & Co.).
Grenier, B.
    1972   *Capital Punishment. New Material* (Ottawa: Queen's Printer).
Hagarty, W. B.
    1960   Capital Punishment Should be Retained. *Canadian Bar Journal,*
            3: 42-51.
Hearn, P. J. O.
    1956   Criminal Law – Capital Punishment, Corporal Punishment,
            Lotteries, Joint Committee Reports. *Canadian Bar Review,* 34:
            844-855.
Henshell, R. L., and Carey, S. H.
    1972   *Deviance, Deterrence and Knowledge of Sanctions.* Paper.
            Eastern Sociological Society Meetings (Boston: April).
House of Commons, Great Britain
    1964   *Parliamentary Debates.,* 704: 882.
Hughes, E.
    1972   Analysis of Canadian Police Homicides (Unpublished Manuscript.
            University of Ottawa).
Inbau, F. E., and Carrington, F. G.
    1971   The Case of the So-Called Hard Line Approach to Crime. *Ann.
            Amer. Acad. Pol. Soc. Sci.,* 397: 19-27.
Jayewardene, C. H. S.
    1960   Criminal Homicide (Unpublished Ph. D. Disseration. University of
            Pennsylvania).
    1961   The Death Penalty in Ceylon. *Ceylon Jour. Hist. Soc. Stud.,* 3:
            166-186.

1964   Are Murderers Dangerous? *Prob. Child Care Jour.*, 2: 33-35.
1964   Criminal Homicide in Ceylon. *Prob. Child Care Jour.*, 3: 15-30.
1969   The Measurement of Criminal Homicide. *Prob. Child Care Jour.*,
        7: 1-4.
1971   *Value Change of Emergent Youth in Ceylon.* Paper. Conference
        on Population Growth, the Human Condition and Politics in South
        East Asia. 1970-1980. New York, Columbia University: November.
1972   The Canadian Movement Against the Death Penalty. *Canad. Jour.
        Criminol. Correct.*, 14: 366-391.
1972   *Homicide and Punishment: A Study in Deterrence.* Paper. Learned
        Societies of Canada. Montreal.

Jayewardene, C. H. S., and Ranasinghe, H.
1963   *Criminal Homicide in the Southern Province* (Colombo: Colombo
        Apothecaries Co. Ltd.).

Joint Committee of the Senate and House of Commons on Capital and
Corporal Punishment and Lotteries
1955   *Minutes of Proceedings and Evidence Witness: J. Alex Edmison*
        (Ottawa: Queen's Printer).
1955   *Minutes of Proceedings and Evidence Appendix F* (Ottawa: Queen's
        Printer).
1956   *Report* (Ottawa: Queen's Printer).

Jones, J. A.
1924   *Pioneer Crimes and Punishments* (Toronto: George N. Morang).

Judicial Committee on Capital Punishment Pertaining to the Problems of the
Death Penalty and its Administration in California
1957   Report of the Subcommittee. *Assembly Interim Committee Reports.
        1955-1957.* Vol. 20, No. 3, p. 12.

Kidman, J.
1947   *The Canadian Prison* (Toronto: The Ryerson Press).

Kingston Whig Standard
1972   March 9th.

Knight, M.
1964   The Irish Criminal Justice Act. 1964. *Justice Peace Loc. Govmn.
        Rev.*, 127: 674-676.

Kuykendall, H. K.
1969   The Deterrent Efficacy of Punishment (Unpublished Master's Thesis.
        University of Texas).

L'Action
1967   October 23rd.

La Presse
1971   August 16th.

Lawes, L.
1932   *Twenty Thousand Years in Sing Sing* (New York: R. Long and R. R.
        Smith).

Leader Post
    1971   March 18th.
Le Devoir
    1971   October 29th, November 20th.
Lomer, A. R. M.
    1958   *Canadians in the Making* (Toronto: Longmans Green and Co.).
Macdonald, J. M.
    1961   *The Murderer and His Victim* (Springfield, Ill.: C. C. Thomas).
MacDonald, L.
    1967   Crime and Punishment in Canada. A Statistical Test of the Conventional Wisdom. *Canad. Rev. Sociol. Anthropol.,* 6: 212-236.
    1971   Is the Crime Rate Increasing? In C. L. Boydell, G. F. Grindstaff, and P. C. Whitehead, *Critical Issues in Canadian Society* (Toronto: Holt, Rinehart & Winston of Canada Ltd.) 467-478.
Mattick, H. W.
    1966   *The Unexamined Death* (Chicago: John Howard Association).
McCafferty, J. A.
    1954   Capital Punishment in the United States 1930-1952 (Unpublished M. A. Thesis. Ohio State University).
McGrath, W. T.
    1956   *Should Canada Abolish the Gallows and the Lash?* (Winnipeg: Stovel Advocate Press).
Moh, H.
    1873   *Shall Capital Punishment be Abolished?* (Montreal: Daniel Rose).
Montreal Star
    1972   February 1st, February 2nd.
Morris, T., and Cooper, L. Blom
    1964   *A Calendar of Murder* (London: Michael Joseph).
Morton, J. D.
    1959   Murder Most Foul. *Canad. Bar Jour.,* 2: 114-120.
Mulvihill, D. J., Tumin, M. M., and Curtis, L. A.
    1969   *Crimes of Violence* (Washington, D. C.: Government Printing Office).
Newell, W. B.
    1965   *Crime and Justice among the Iroquois Indians* (Montreal: Caughanawaga Historical Society).
Newman, P.
    1965   *Malaria Eradication and Population Growth* (Ann Arbor, Mich.: School of Public Health, University of Michigan).
Normandeau, A.
    1964   La Peine de Mort au Canada. *Rev. Droit pen. criminol.,* 46: 547-559.
Ohio Adult Parole Authority
    1966   *Summary of Parole Performances of First Degree Murderers in*

Ohio for the Calendar Year 1965 (Columbus).

Ottawa Citizen
  1961   *Capital Punishment. A Collection of News, Views and Comments
         as they appeared during January 1960 in the pages of the Ottawa
         Citizen* (Ottawa: Ottawa Citizen).
  1965   June 25th.
  1966   March 7th.
  1971   November 8th, December 18th.
  1973   January 22nd, February 6th, February 10th, February 11th,
         March 17th.

Ottawa Journal
  1971   March 17th.
  1972   January 4th, January 14th.
  1973   January 20th, January 27th, January 30th, February 3rd, February
         17th.

Patrick, C. H.
  1965   The Status of Capital Punishment. A World Perspective. *Jour. Crim.
         Law Criminol.*, 56: 397-411.

Pennsylvania Board of Parole
  1961   *A Comparison of Releases and Recidivists from June 1, 1946, to
         May 31, 1961* (Harrisburg).

President's Commission on Law Enforcement and Administration of Justice
  1967   *The Challenge of Crime in a Free Society* (Washington, D.C.:
         Government Printing Office).
  1967   *Task Force Report: Science and Technology* (Washington, D.C.:
         Government Printing Office).

Quebec Chronicle
  1923   March 7th.

Reckless, W. C.
  1969   The Use of the Death Penalty. *Crime Delinq.*, 15: 43-56.

Riddell, W. R.
  1925   Criminal Courts and Law in Early (Upper) Canada. *Ontario Histori-
         cal Society's Papers and Records*, 22: 3-14.

Robin, G. D.
  1963   Justifiable Homicides by Police Officers. *Jour. Crim. Law Criminol.*,
         54: 225-231.
  1967   Justifiable Homicides by Police Officers. In M. E. Wolfgang: *Studies
         in Homicide* (New York: Harper and Row) 88-100.

Rokeach, M.
  1960   *The Open and Closed Mind. Investigation into the Nature of Belief
         Systems and Personality Systems* (New York: Basic Books).
  1969   *Beliefs, Attitudes and Values. A Theory of Organization and Change*
         (San Francisco: Jassey-Bass).

Royal Commission on Capital Punishment
    1954   *Evidence 30th Day. Witness: Professor Thorsten Sellin. 1st*
            February (London: H.M.S.O.).
    1954   *Report* (London: H.M.S.O.).
Savitz, L. D.
    1958   A Study of Capital Punishment. *Jour. Crim. Law Criminol.*,
            49: 338-341.
Schuessler, K. F.
    1952   The Deterrent Influence of the Death Penalty. *Ann. Amer. Acad.*
            Pol. Soc. Sci., 284: 54-62.
Schull, J.
    1971   *Rebellion* (Toronto: Macmillan of Canada).
Sellin, T.
    1932   Common Sense and the Death Penalty. *Pris. Jour.* (Oct) 12.
    1937   *Research Memorandum on Crime in the Depression* (New York:
            Social Science Research Council).
    1955   Homicides in Retentionist and Abolitionist States. In Joint Com-
            mittee of the Senate and House on Capital and Corporal Punish-
            ment and Lotteries: *Minutes of Proceedings and Evidence.*
            Appendix F (Ottawa: Queen's Printer).
    1959   *The Death Penalty. A Report for the Model Penal Code Project*
            of the American Law Institute (Philadelphia: American Law
            Institute).
    1961   Capital Punishment. *Fed. Prob.,* 15: 3-11.
    1964   Death and Imprisonment as Deterrents to Murder. In H. A.
            Bedeau: *The Death Penalty in America* (Garden City, N.Y.:
            Anchor Doubleday) 274-284.
    1964   Capital Punishment. In D. Dressler: *Readings in Criminology and*
            Penology (New York: Columbia University Press).
    1965   The Inevitable End of Capital Punishment. *Crim. Law Quart.,* 8:
            36-51.
    1965   Homicides and Assaults in American Prisons. *Acta Criminol. Med.*
            Leg. Jap., 31: 1-4.
    1967   Homicide in Retentionist and Abolitionist States. In T. Sellin:
            Capital Punishment (New York: Harper and Row) 135-138.
    1967   Death Penalty and Police Safety. In T. Sellin: *Capital Punishment*
            (New York: Harper and Row) 138-153.
    1967   Prison Homicides. In T. Sellin: *Capital Punishment* (New York:
            Harper and Row) 154-196.
Shaw, E. S.
    1960   *A Companion to Murder* (London: Cassel).
Sheppard, C. S.
    1971   Towards a Better Understanding of the Violent Offender. *Canad.*

            Jour. Criminol. Correct., 13: 60-67.

Singh, A.
    1973   Criminal Homicide and Culture Conflict in Canada (Unpublished
            M.A. Thesis, University of Ottawa).

Smith, G. B.
    1958   Situational Murder due to Emotional Stress. *Jour. Soc. Ther.,* 4,
            173-181.

Sonopresse Survey
    1971   August 14th.

Stanton, J. M.
    1969   Murderers on Parole. *Crime Delinq.,* 15: 149-155.

State of New York Executive Department
    1964   *34th Annual Report of the Division of Parole for 1963* (Albany).

Statistics Canada
    1973   *Murder Statistics 1961-1970* (Ottawa: Queen's Printer).
    1973   *Police Administration Statistics 1971* (Ottawa: Queen's Printer).

Tarde, G.
    1912   *Penal Philosophy* (Boston: Little, Brown).

Taylor, E. L. H.
    1958   A Secular Revolution in Christian Disguise. *Canadian Bar Journal,*
            1: 41-46.

Teevan, J. J.
    1972   Deterrent Effects of Punishment: The Canadian Case. *Canad. Jour.*
            Criminol. Correct., 14: 68-82.

Telegram
    1946   May 17th.

The Gazette
    1920   October 4th.
    1921   December 27th.
    1922   February 24th.
    1923   March 2nd.
    1971   February 27th, August 17th, October 15th.
    1972   January 18th, February 1st, February 2nd.

The Star
    1946   July 13th.
    1953   January 5th.

Thomas, D. S.
    1927   *Social Aspects of the Business Cycle* (New York: A.A. Knopf).

Tittle, C. R.
    1969   Crime Rates and Legal Sanctions. *Soc. Prob.,* 16: 409-423.

Toby, J.
    1964   Is Punishment Necessary? *Jour. Crim. Law Criminol.,* 55: 332-
            337.

Truro Daily News
   1972   January 17th.
Tuttle, E. A.
   1961   *The Crusade Against Capital Punishment* (London: Stevens and
          Stevens).
United Church of Canada
   1960   *Alternatives to Capital Punishment* (Toronto: United Church of
          Canada. Board of Evangelism and Social Service).
United Kingdom
   1964   *Hansard.*
United Nations
   1960   *Capital Punishment* (New York: United Nations).
   1965   *Capital Punishment* (New York: United Nations).
   1967   *Demographic Yearbook* (New York: United Nations).
Verkko, V.
   1951   *Homicides and Suicides in Finland and their Dependency on National
          Character* (Copenhagen: G.E. Gads Forlag).
Vold, G. B.
   1932   Can the Death Penalty Prevent Crime? *Pris. Jour.* (Oct.), 3-7.
Wolfgang, M. E.
   1958   *Patterns of Criminal Homicide* (Philadelphia: University of Penn-
          sylvania Press).
Ziesel, H.
   1968   *Some Data on Jury Attitudes toward Capital Punishment* (Chicago:
          University of Chicago. Center for Studies in Criminal Justice).
Zimring, F. E.
   1971   *Perspectives on Deterrence* (Washington, D.C.: Government Printing
          Office).

Index

Index

About the Author

C.H.S. Jayewardene is a forensic pathologist and criminologist with the M.B. degree from the University of Ceylon and the Ph.D. in sociology and criminology from the University of Pennsylvania. His main interest is the study of violence with special emphasis on its cultural aspects. However, Dr. Jayewardene is the author of a number of books and articles on a wide variety of topics varying from criminality among the Eskimos to fertility and mortality among the Ceylonese. He is at present professor in and chairman of the Department of Criminology of the University of Ottawa.